WELCOME HOME

Also by Sandra Ingerman
SOUL RETRIEVAL

WELCOME HOME

FOLLOWING YOUR SOUL'S JOURNEY HOME

SANDRA INGERMAN

HarperOne
An Imprint of HarperCollinsPublishers

HarperOne

HarperCollins books may be purchased for educational, business, or
sales promotional use. For information please write: Special Markets
Department, HarperCollins Publishers, 10 East 53rd Street, New
York, NY 10022.

HarperCollins Web site: http://www.harpercollins.com
HarperCollins®, 🏭®, and HarperOne™ are trademarks of
HarperCollins Publishers.

Library of Congress Cataloging-in-Publication Data
Ingerman, Sandra.
     Welcome home : following your soul's journey home / Sandra
Ingerman. —1st ed.
     Includes index.
     ISBN 978–0–06–250267–4
     1. Spiritual healing.   2. Mental healing.   3. Shamanism.
4. Diaries—Authorship—Religious aspects.   I. Title.
Bl65.M4I453   1994
131—dc20   93–4429

          09 10 11 12 RRD(H) 20 19 18 17 16

*For
Easy Hill
and
Smokey*

CONTENTS

WELCOME HOME

INTRODUCTION

Welcome Home: Following Your Soul's Journey Home is for all people who are ready to move away from their past woundedness and refocus their energy on creating a positive present and future.

If you have been on a healing journey for a while—whether through traditional or alternative counseling, spiritual methods, or traditional or alternative physical healing—this book is for you. Do you know that there is life after healing? Do you know how to shift out of an illness model to create your life differently than you have in the past?

Welcome Home addresses the issues that we need to examine as we change the direction of our lives—it is a guide for shifting our focus to the present and the future. Each chapter includes step-by-step exercises that will help you tap into your own creative potential. This is a book that you should read at your own pace, taking the actions appropriate for you at the end of each chapter.

Welcome Home is about taking responsibility for creating a better future. No one is going to do it for you—not the government, not organized religion, not science, and certainly not a mothership from outer space. You must be personally responsible for creating a positive future for yourself and this planet. This means clarifying who you are and what your gifts, strengths, and belief systems are and then making changes in your life. It means becoming your own authority and taking action—now!

This book allows no place for guilt, judgment, or blame, which are all associated with the illness model. We are looking at a life in which energy is directed toward healthy ways of being that allow us to make choices and to grow. You have made the choice to read this book. When you don't agree with me or you don't understand what I am saying, you can simply recognize that. You can embrace the information that makes sense and serves you in your growth process, and you can ignore any information that is not part of your journey now.

Healing is in many ways a lifelong process, and those of us who have been in the therapy loop and in a healing process for some time must decide whether it is time to redirect our energy. This book is for people who have already done much of their healing work; it is not for those who have not yet begun. We can't deny that there are wounds in our past; but at a certain point, each of us must stand up and say, "I have different tools available to me now. I have done enough work on what went wrong, and it's time to focus on making life right."

Welcome Home: Following Your Soul's Journey Home addresses several themes:

- Envisioning a future by redirecting our creative energies away from the illness of the past to the healthy needs of the present and future

- Receiving healing energy from the Universe

- Having passion for life

- Raising our awareness of how we communicate and treat others on an energy level

- Setting boundaries between ourselves and others as we tap into our creativity and vision

- Letting go of limiting beliefs from the past, thus freeing our creativity

- Staying centered in times of change by developing a strong identity

- Creating a positive future by knowing ourselves and re-membering the gifts and talents we brought into this world

- Understanding our own creative power and not expect-ing an outside force to make things better for us

- Expressing our own soul

- Leaving human law to return to nature and its cycles

- Moving from self-focus to a more global focus

- Bringing honesty, integrity, and compassion back into our personal relationships and business communities

- Healing some of the scars we have left on the earth.

This is not a book about shamanism, although I will share some shamanic practices with you. This book comes from what I have learned in my own shamanic journeys, in working with clients, and in teaching workshops. What you need to know about shamanism to understand what I am talking about here is included in the chapters that follow. For readers who want a deeper understanding of shamanism, the appendix provides an explanation of some of the basic principles.

This book is written for people who have been on various healing paths. Because my own background is in shamanic coun-seling and healing, many of my case studies will include sha-manic experiences. The individuals who appear in the case studies are composites created from real situations; they do not represent specific individuals. But please realize that all healing paths bring us to the same place. This book starts where healing practices leave off: how to continue with our own lives and spiritual paths after the healing has occurred, whatever method was used.

The system of shamanism is a path to accessing spiritual information, and I share some of the teachings that come to me from my spiritual teacher, Isis. I originally met Isis a few years ago when I felt the need to go on a vision quest. Although my own shamanic journeying gives me much of the guidance I need, I wanted some time alone to allow a vision of where my path was heading.

I began to work with a Native American man who was going to facilitate my vision quest. He asked me to fast on only fruit for thirty days before I went out for my vision. Because of the fast, I found myself entering into a semi-altered state even before the vision quest began. About a week before the time for my quest, he called to say he had broken his foot and would not be able to facilitate my work.

I was already on my vision quest, so canceling was out of the question. I finally found a woman who would take over and went out to her home in the country, ready to do my vision quest in a strict way. I was planning on being out and awake in nature for four days and three nights. The woman asked me to stay flexible and not to have such rigid rules about how to be during this time. When I told her that I wanted to work in a traditional way, she assured me that there was no rigid traditional way. To teach me about flexibility, she marked my sitting circle with blue corn for one acre around. (In a typical vision quest the circle is just big enough to include the person's sitting body.)

In July in northern New Mexico, the weather is quite hot. Between fasting on fruit for one month and now having no food or water, I was entering a very altered state. I sat quietly and patiently waiting for something to happen. By midday I had been stung by an insect, though I never saw what stung me, and I had a huge welt on my arm. A few hours later, still in the heat of the day, I saw a vision of a very old Native American grandmother walking toward me. She said, "If you want a vision, go into the sweat lodge on this land and go to sleep. Your vision will come in a dream."

I struggled for a while with this information. I still had such a rigid idea about how my vision was supposed to come—sleep was not part of my plan. I finally decided to give in to the instructions I had received, and I entered the sweat lodge that was within my one-acre circle. It was so wonderful to get out of the heat and lie down on the cool dirt floor beneath me. I stayed there until nightfall, when I went to sleep. Isis appeared to me in a dream and said, "I am returning to the planet at this time to restore peace, harmony, and balance." Throughout the next few days she began to give me instructions in my dreams. From that day forth, she has given me a great wealth of information, including the clear instruction to shift my focus to working with the future: "The world is looking so bleak. Provide a bright spot, be a window of light that people can look into."

I realize that now I sometimes go to the extreme in being future-oriented; however, I feel strongly that we need more balance in our lives; we have become too directed toward dealing with the past.

I challenge you to focus on creating a brighter future. I honor your process and who you are, and I trust that you will use only that information which is helpful to you now.

My power animal also had a message about *Welcome Home: Following Your Soul's Journey Home*. When I went to meet him in the Lower World, the territory of the parallel universe I enter to speak with him, I found him waiting for me with tears in his eyes. He said, "Please bring joy into the world."

How to Use This Book

I wrote this book to help individuals move out of the healing process and into following their soul's journey. It is also meant for helping professionals who are looking for ways to facilitate their clients' shift to a focus on the present and the future. Readers can use the information in the book and do the exercises in each chapter individually. These exercises can also be done by a group of people who share a similar focus. If you have been studying shamanism and shamanic journeying, you can do the exercises in a group where the participants journey to access the information requested. If you have not been involved in shamanic journeying, you can still do the exercises with other people with whom you can share your process.

If you are a helping professional, try the exercises with your clients and patients who are ready to move away from the past. You will find useful information on setting boundaries in your work with others. Setting boundaries effectively can prevent the common problem of burnout in the helping professions.

I ask only that all exercises be done from a place of self-love and compassion for all living beings on the planet.

CHAPTER 1

PLANT A SEED
AND IT WILL GROW

Siempre awakens with a start. What does she hear? What are those words? What are they trying to tell her? She gets up. She is very groggy. In the darkness she opens her closet and finds her drum.

She tiptoes back to her bed. Why is she being so quiet? There is no one here to wake. She moves slowly and quietly so she won't break the spell of the dream state she has entered.

She climbs into bed and begins to drum. A light swirls around her, and invisible shapes dance before her. She dives downward into the invisible world, leaving her ordinary consciousness behind. The veil between the worlds falls. What was once dark is now light. Her teacher stands before her.

"You've been putting out a call to the spirits for help, for an understanding of how to heal the earth. Your call has been heard. The question is, How committed are you to this path?"

Siempre stands before a teacher who embraces the energy of timelessness. Her beauty is awe-inspiring. Her gaze burns away all lies and illusion; it demands truth. She is Isis.

Siempre looks into her dark eyes. She knows her soul has been seen, and only an answer of pure honesty will be accepted. Siempre clears her throat, raises her chin, and straightens her posture, trying to embody the power and presence of the Goddess who stands before her. She answers, "Yes, I give my life to follow this path. I am devoted to the healing of the earth."

Two years ago I felt a call to write this book, *Welcome Home: Following Your Soul's Journey Home,* and the story I've just told was "given" to me. Since the planting of that seed, the story has been growing inside me. So I now continue with my story as Siempre's journey becomes my own.

"What kind of future are you creating if you are stuck in the woundedness of the past?" In a deep sleep I heard these words resound. This question from a voice without any identity disturbed my rest. As I drifted in and out of the sleep state, I repeated it to myself: "What kind of future are you creating if you are stuck in the woundedness of the past?" These words were a powerful message for me, but I also found myself disturbed by them. I suddenly realized that as a community—as a society—we as human beings are not creating a future for this planet. What most of the people in the world around me are doing is re-creating the same abuses that they say they want to heal. We might re-create dysfunctional relationships with our friends and partners, in our workplaces, or in our communities that remind us of those who wounded us in the past. We might also find ourselves re-creating abusive behavior toward ourselves and others that reminds us of what we had to endure as children. The earth has been providing a stage for the dramas of our individual histories to be played out again.

As I thought about this, I came totally awake. There was just a hint of light, letting me know that morning would come soon. What a magical time! It is so still outside. There is no noise of traffic to disturb me. There are no other voices to invade my thoughts. Even the psychic airwaves are quiet as the people who live nearby are still lost to their dreams. The lack of visible and invisible noise and activity allows me to sink down and travel to the places inside myself where no one can intrude. I feel almost as if I alone inhabit the earth. I can be alone with my thoughts, with no voices to judge me. Even my critical mind has not yet awakened.

In my work as a shamanic practitioner and teacher of shamanism, I listen again and again to stories of hurt and abuse. It is hard to imagine what people have endured in their lives, and I find myself continually honoring people's courage as they confront the past abuse in their lives in order to heal. But I often become frustrated when I hear clients repeat stories of their past over and over, as if these are in some way all they have to offer. I sometimes find myself questioning the importance of this repetition. One obvious reason for it is the hope that retelling a story about past trauma will bring resolution. But while I was teaching a recent workshop, I began to wonder about this.

I was sitting at lunch, talking to some friends about my desire to travel to where my family originates in order to trace my roots. My family as I know it is part of the New World. My grandparents emigrated from the Ukraine before World War II. When my family first came to the United States, they maintained some contact with those they had left behind. But at some point, all contact stopped. My mother and aunts and uncles all seem to remember different reasons for this lack of communication. The point, however, is that I have no knowledge of my family's history.

When I speak to my friends about how this feels to me, I hear a voice inside my head say, "People who don't know the history of their family and their roots have no other story to tell except their own personal history. People whose own history is one of abuse have only *that* story to tell." I now realize why it is so hard to move a person out of the woundedness of the past. The healing of the planet and those who inhabit it cannot take place until we stop re-creating the stories of the past. Unless we can create new stories, we are doomed to more illness and trauma.

Do people know that there is more to life than what they have already experienced? Do they even know where to begin in creating a new story? Once we have been on a healing path for a while, gathering pieces of ourselves that left us along the way, we have a great deal of potential for creating something different from what we experienced in our past. We are older now and have different options available than we did when we were young. As adults we have different tools available to us. And we have a responsibility to ourselves—and to all life on the planet— to behave in a life-supportive way. But the information we need in order to do this may not be easily available to us. What if we don't know about the people who went before us, trying to create better lives for themselves and their families? What if we don't know our roots, know the gifts and strengths inherent in our bloodline? We have to begin again.

As I lay in bed that night, my head swimming with ideas and questions, I decided to consult with my teacher for understanding. I picked up my deerskin drum from beside the bed and began to drum the monotonous beat that allows me to slow my brain waves down enough to gain access to the invisible world that exists around me. I feel the familiar tug on my solar plexus that pulls my soul up to a realm of calm and partial darkness where I can meet Isis. I couldn't see her clearly, but I knew by the feeling in my body that I had arrived at the home of my teacher.

I felt her warm glow around me. I began to speak. "Isis, tell me about the future."

She sat down and pondered this request for a moment, then began to speak. "People of your time do not comprehend that all answers lie within each person. It is really not necessary to seek answers from others. That is a giving away of power. People also give away power when they turn to others for a definition of reality. Whatever you believe, you create. So if you think that there is a scarcity of food, love, or money, for example, you will find yourself creating situations that will reflect that belief back to you. People of your time often say, 'You can create your own reality,' without having the slightest idea what this truly means. The words take away the power of this concept. At some point you must realize that all of what one sees and experiences, both positive and negative, is a mass creation by all human beings. It is important to think about what kind of experience you want to have in your future. Do you want to live on a planet where there is a scarcity of food, water, love? Or do you want to live where there is an abundance of nurturance for all life forms? This kind of a world is possible. But it might not lie in the experience of the people of this time. Most people get stuck in the experience of what they have and don't have instead of realizing that there are other possibilities. This is the first thing you need to understand about the future.

"People have more creative power than they realize, so much creative potential that is not being used. Creativity is about using your imagination to envision a healthy and happy life. Instead, you channel that energy into re-creating the past. Use your imagination! In your wildest dreams, what would you want your world to look like? To speak of catastrophic prophesies is just an excuse for not wanting to create things differently. I get so confused about why people want to create such awful images of things to be endured. Why does all life on the planet have to suffer because of your limited imaginations? It brings me great sadness to see this.

In my life, there was so much beauty on the earth around us! All that was built had the breath of life blown into it. Every structure was alive and exuded an energy that was felt by all who entered it. Your structures today are so dead and empty! You should be healed by the buildings you live in. You should stand in awe of the beauty of your creations.

"So my advice to you and the people who live around you is to step back from your life. Use your imagination to envision what you would like your life to be like. Try to imagine what joy and happiness feel like. Reach back to at least one experience in which you felt happy. What situations and experiences do you think would help you regain those feelings? Trust yourself and have faith that you can create this feeling again in your life. You will have to make changes, and as you already know, all change involves taking a risk. But if you don't let fear block your sight, then you must know that you are moving in a positive direction. Life does not end with death. Death is a transition, not an end. So you will be coming back to this earth again. Start thinking now about what you want to come back to."

This last statement set me back some. I thanked Isis for this wealth of information, then turned around and carefully retraced the steps of my journey. I returned to my body feeling centered and present. I opened my eyes and looked around my room. I had a strong desire to get up and leave my bedroom. The confinement of the walls felt claustrophobic—I went outside for some air.

I had totally forgotten about eternity. My thoughts about life had become narrowed by my daily routine and my beliefs about what I must do for survival. I began to realize how much I limit myself and how lost I had become in linear time.

I had been working at a very fast pace trying to heal myself and to help others to heal. I was obsessed with wanting to see a totally new world in my lifetime. I had become so lost in this goal that I had forgotten that *there is no end*.

I needed to find a way to expand my view of life again and go to a deeper place inside myself. I knew I had had that experience before, and I found myself questioning how I had lost it. I had become so caught up in daily life that I had forgotten an important message that I had received from Isis quite a long time before: *You must get away from the laws of man and get back to the laws of nature.*

It was hard to continue my counseling practice after I understood this statement. For what was the underlying complaint of most of my clients? Don't most people complain about a "lack of"? Scarcity seems to be the basis for how people see life. But is scarcity a natural problem? When I searched for a deeper understanding of nature, I realized that nature provides an abundance of all things; however, one must recognize how the cycles of the season, the cycles of the moon, the cycles of the sun, and the time of day provide abundance. This knowledge felt far away from the artificial cycles set up by modern living, in which the cycles of nature are rarely observed. What has become important instead is linear time, where we are ruled by clocks.

It was at this point that I realized I had been holding my breath. I started to walk, to try to become more aware of my breath. I decided that the best place for me to be was in my garden. Within moments of aligning myself with the energy of the new growth in my garden, I would get the help I needed to slow down and recenter myself. It was late spring, and there were many varieties of vegetables, herbs, and trees growing. I opened the gate to the garden and started down the stone path.

I decided to sit down on the path itself rather than on the wooden bench where I usually go for the early morning sun while I drink my coffee. It felt more appropriate that day to sit directly on the ground—to try to let go of all the thoughts that arose from my dreams and journey through the early hours of the morning. I needed to find that place of calm inside. As I sat cross-legged with my eyes closed, feeling the warmth of the sun on my body, I became aware of a hum around me. What was this noise? I had thought I was alone. I opened my eyes and looked around but didn't see anyone. Trying to regain my center, I took a deep breath and closed my eyes again. Once again I heard a hum, so I continued to listen with my eyes closed. I am used to hearing things when I am quiet. My drum is one path to the invisible world; the deep silence inside myself is another. A message came to me after I had listened to this gentle and soothing hum for a while: "This is the hum of new life." I realized I was listening to all the new plants and trees in the garden humming. What an incredible sound—the sound of healthy life! I wonder if all life has a hum, whether one can tell by the hum how healthy a person is?

I knew I had a lot to learn here.

What kind of future are we creating if we are stuck in the woundedness of the past?

We are all coming back. Start thinking now about what you want to come back to.

Keep your power. Don't give it away by allowing other people to define reality.

We live in an abundant Universe.

It is time to return our attention to the laws and cycles of nature.

We have the potential to create a positive future.

There is a "hum" to life.

A thought to ponder:

Plant a seed and it will grow.

EXERCISES

1. Let your imagination wander. What would you like your future to look and feel like? Use a blank page to jot down notes to yourself or draw a picture. Or draw something that symbolizes what you want your life to be like.

We will do more with this exercise as we proceed. This is just a beginning.

2. Who do you count on to give you a definition of reality? Make a list and evaluate how true the information you have received from those people has been.

CHAPTER 2

A STORY
OF PASSION

I work with a system of spiritual healing called shamanism. A shamanic practitioner journeys to the spiritual realms on the client's behalf to gather information on the appropriate method of healing in a particular case. I use shamanism for my personal teaching as well as on behalf of my community.

One of the healing methods I use is soul retrieval. With this method, the shamanic practitioner retrieves any life essence that has been lost by a client due to an emotional or physical trauma. Loss of a part of the soul can create an "opening" in a person where an illness might enter. Some people experiencing soul loss may complain about feeling empty or not "all here." As all shamans around the world know, when a trauma happens, a person actually loses a piece of the self. This loss of essence or life force is necessary for survival. A person who stayed fully present in the body at the time of the trauma might not be able to survive the experience. It is the role of the shaman to track down that person's soul or essence later in nonordinary reality and physically return it to the body.

I work with people who have experienced many varieties of trauma, although I often have reservations about working with people with serious illnesses (a topic I will discuss further later in the chapter). I am not afraid of the illness itself. I have complete trust in my helping spirits and know that as long as I work with them, I have nothing to worry about. The power of helping spirits one draws on in shamanism represents the power of the Universe. So I do not use my own energy; I am the hands and heart and mind of the spirits I work with. For my own personal growth, I have teachers in human form in nonordinary reality who help me develop my own consciousness. When I am working with clients in a healing manner, I utilize the spirit of an animal that gives me directions and power. Before I begin, I ask my clients if there is any history about past traumas or abuses they want to share. I have found in my experience of doing shamanic journeying for people that I can now go further with my work if I have a deeper starting point. When I journey "cold" with no information from my clients, a good portion of the journey involves establishing the client's history instead of looking at what needs to happen for a healing to occur. I now try to get a person's history before I start my work so I can go straight to the problem.

This is a switch from how I worked with people in the beginning. The shaman must have total trust in her helping spirits; the shaman and the spirits she works with must be a strong team. When I first started doing soul retrieval work, I needed to understand *how* my spirits could help me. I knew that I could trust them, but I didn't yet understand how the process of soul retrieval worked. In my earlier soul retrievals, I found it was better to have as little information as possible to journey with; that way, if I received information from the spirits that really spoke to my client's past, I didn't have to wonder if I had received the information from the spirits or already knew it from the client. I spent the first few years establishing trust in the process and in myself.

Now that the bond of trust is strong between me and my power animal, I find myself letting my work evolve to a deeper place. I already know that I can spend the first part of my shamanic journey quizzing my power animal on details of a client's problem that can be corroborated later by my client, but I choose not to waste any precious time in the journeying process in a superficial discussion with my power animal.

In soul retrieval, the challenge for me and for my clients is the same. Both of us have to be receptive to the power of the Universe for any healing to be successful. If I use my own energy during the work, I will probably find myself drained and might eventually become ill. If I open to the power of the Universe and receive the healing energy but my client is not receptive, the healing might not be successful. Because it is so important, I have been spending a lot of time in both the dream state and the waking state looking at the issue of receptivity; the ability to receive is crucial in all areas of one's life. In doing shamanic work, I must be willing to receive the power of the Universe. Anyone getting a healing must be willing to receive the power and energy of the healing.

When Anne, who was suffering from the post-traumatic stress of a car accident, came to see me, she complained that life had not been the same for her since she drove her car off the road and crashed into a tree. In Anne's case, I did not have to go very far back into time looking for her soul part. Her accident had taken place only six months prior to my work with her.

For a soul retrieval, I will ask Anne to lie down next to me on my rug in the small room in which I work. I will touch her at the shoulder, hip, and ankle so that the psychic connection between the two of us is strong. I use a tape of drumming so that my own free soul can leave my body and search for Anne's soul. If the soul gets shocked out of the body, we begin to feel pulled to that soul. We cannot concentrate all our energy on being here and in the present because we are being pulled out of our bodies to a piece of ourselves that we lost in the past. No wonder most of us cannot let go of our pasts—parts of our soul are stuck in unresolved traumas.

Indigenous cultures understood this phenomenon. If a person had an accident, became ill, or had a traumatic experience with another human being, the shaman went in search of the lost soul and returned it. But in our modern world, where only what can be seen and statistically proven is valid, spiritual illness is no longer recognized. So I often find myself searching back ten, twenty, thirty, sometimes sixty or seventy years looking for lost soul parts. What a journey! How awful for people to be separated from their vitality for that long! No wonder so much in our society is dysfunctional. People are disconnected from themselves, no longer aware of who they are, of their own self-truth, no longer on a path forward but constantly being drawn back psychically into the past.

But Anne's challenge was not so great. She heard of my work and came to me soon after her accident, knowing that she had lost a piece of herself in the car wreck.

After I explained the method of soul retrieval to Anne, she asked, "Why doesn't my soul come back on its own? Why can't I do this work myself?"

I am often asked this question. In some instances the soul does return on its own. But sometimes it gets lost in the parallel universe that it flees to, and in that case, outside intervention is needed. It also sometimes happens that the soul is afraid to come back, especially if it is a part that was abused at an early age and doesn't know that it is safe to come back now. Or maybe the soul has actually been stolen. Another person may take a piece of our essence to remain in connection with us, or someone may try to steal our power or energy. If Anne had told me she felt great and more "here" after her car wreck, I would have assumed that the soul part had returned on its own. But the fact that she had a complaint, that she had felt lost and "spaced out" since the wreck, indicated she was suffering from soul loss.

Sometimes people have spontaneous healings—and these are a gift from the spirits—but that does not seem to be the norm.

Usually the soul part is lost or resists coming back or has been stolen by another person.

I explained to Anne that getting her soul back would be a very sacred experience. She looked around my room. It was very bright, with light streaming in through the windows, and brightly colored animals, candles, and rocks gave it a childlike quality. Anne didn't understand why but said she felt a sense of peacefulness and safety. As she closed her eyes and took a deep breath, she said she felt the presence of Spirit. Although Anne had just met me that morning, she felt safe with me. She said she understood my explanation of soul loss and shamanism and that it all sounded right and familiar, even though she had never encountered the concept of soul retrieval work before. She trusted me and was very happy to be with me doing the work. She realized that she did not understand enough about what had happened to her to attempt this work on her own. She felt ready.

Once Anne's feeling of safety and confidence was established, I reviewed the process of soul retrieval. I would lie down next to her and listen to a drumming tape, which would allow my free soul to leave my body and search for her soul in nonordinary reality.

"Tracking your soul is the easy part for me because I have my helping spirits to rely on for this part of the work. The difficult part is maintaining the concentration that I need to actually transfer your soul part from nonordinary reality into ordinary reality—holding a tangible piece of you in my hands, maintaining concentration, and then blowing that piece of you back into your body again."

"What can I do to help?" she asked.

"Just stay as psychically open as you can," I replied. "Try to let me see what happened to you at the time of the accident. Don't block me."

I knew that despite what she said, on an unconscious level she might not follow my instructions. If Anne was not ready for this healing to take place or if unconsciously she didn't really feel safe with me, she would shut down, making the job of tracking her soul much more difficult for me and my helping spirits. By making this statement, I was just planting a seed.

I reminded her, "Don't forget that a healing is about to take place. I am getting ready to return your vital soul to you, so please keep your awareness on preparing yourself to receive your soul back."

In the past few years I have had many dreams about this particular instruction. Being a person who gets so much of my spiritual information in an auditory way, I often get important messages through words in my dreams. For years now I have been hearing a recurring message; in my dream I am told, "The success of any healing is the ability of the client to receive the healing." Every time I have this dream, I seem to receive it differently. The first time I heard the words only. I thought it was an interesting concept, but it didn't hit very deep inside me. I received it on only a superficial level.

But last time I had this dream, I really got it. Besides the words, I received the kinesthetic experience of the words. I could feel in the dream state what it was like to receive healing energy. If only I could be that receptive in the waking state! But in my own journey through life, I am constantly working on the issue of receiving. My biggest challenge at this point is to teach my clients what it means to receive a healing.

My work is to plant seeds. I offer an idea and know that the client's unconscious will work with it in its own time. Healing is not just a one-time, instant experience. A healing needs time to deepen. The effects of one healing session can take weeks or months for the client's body and psyche to integrate. I have an absolute trust in each person's timing in receiving the healing, but I am often frustrated because I know how much more powerful the work could be if we could open our hearts and bodies and be more receptive.

It interferes with receptivity when people get trapped in the details of the soul loss event instead of realizing that they are getting their souls back. Part of my role is to remind clients of the true purpose of our work together.

In my journey outside time and space on Anne's behalf, I was successful in locating the piece of her soul that flew out of her body at the time of her car accident. I pulled that part from nonordinary reality into ordinary reality and proceeded to blow the soul back into Anne's heart center and then, after sitting her up, into the crown of her head.

"Welcome home," I said, as I looked into Anne's eyes.

Anne took a deep breath in response. "Thank you," she said as her eyes filled with tears. "You can have no idea how this feels. I feel like a deflated balloon that just got filled up with air."

Her response showed that Anne did indeed receive the healing.

Because, as I have said, being open and receptive is so important to the healing, much of my work is spent preparing the client. One way I help my clients understand that a healing is about to take place and that they must be ready to receive it is to suggest that they ask for a dream about it the night before their session. I instruct them to put out a silent but clear intention—just before going to bed—for a dream that will prepare them for the healing that is about to occur. Even if the conscious mind is not ready, the psyche can be of great help in the dream state.

Another challenge in my work is encouraging people to take responsibility for their own healing. Often, people come to me to get a "spiritual aspirin," a symptomatic cure. I feel strongly that one of the keys to a successful healing is the willingness to look at what was out of balance in a person's life that allowed an illness to occur in the first place. This is why I have reservations about working with someone who is facing a life-threatening illness. There needs to be a strong commitment to look at the cause of the illness—something that cannot be done from a place of guilt—and to assess what changes are needed to prevent illness from returning.

In a session with Mary, who has AIDS, I learned how the issues of receiving the healing and wanting to change one's life figure into the healing process.

Mary came into my office looking extremely pale. There seemed to be little life force around her, and her blue eyes were beginning to dim. My room was chilly, because the cloudy sky that morning prevented any solar heating. (I like the coolness; it keeps me alert to the challenge ahead.)

Mary told me that a friend of hers had recommended that she come to see me. I understood that the disease Mary struggles with keeps her energy low, but I could not get a sense of whether Mary really wanted to be doing this work or exactly why she had come.

I have learned from seriously ill people to be as direct and honest as possible because the stakes are so high.

So I asked, "Mary, do you want to live?"

Mary looked a little shocked by the directness of the question.

I continued, "I just want to get a sense of what our work this morning should be about. For some people, the next step on their healing journey is to be cured of their illness through life. For others, their next step is to be cured by the transition of death. I want to know if, at this point, you have any feelings about your healing process, so I can get a sense of what your intention is."

Mary answered, "I do believe that I want to live."

Mary proceeded to tell me about her past history with illness. She had already healed herself of two life-threatening illnesses. She had confronted death both ten years and five years prior to the onset of AIDS.

I asked Mary if there was any history about her childhood that I should know before journeying on her behalf.

Mary told me that nothing stood out about her past that she felt would be useful information for me. She said there had been no physical abuse in her past but that she had been emotionally abused. I didn't ask Mary for the details; I wanted to leave it to the spirits to show me exactly what Mary's past experience had been. What I did find important was that this was the third life-threatening illness Mary had faced. Clearly, something was going on that needed to be explored.

To prepare Mary for the work that was about to take place, I told her that we would lie on the floor together in physical contact and that I would journey on her behalf to look for any soul parts that would be helpful for her to have back.

I lit a candle to signify my first call to the helping spirits. I picked up my rattle and sang a song that always begins my healing work. The song reminds me of my connection with my power animal and helping spirits, as well as with all of life. But most importantly, singing the song strongly opens my heart and allows me to receive the spiritual help that is about to come. After singing for a few minutes, I saw the image of a little girl. Here was the first soul part. This was my cue to lie down beside Mary and put on the drumming tape.

My free soul floated out of my body through my solar plexus. I drifted back in time to the Middle World, where I met my power animal. We saw Mary riding her tricycle on a suburban street. To both the right and the left, we saw just a glimpse of houses. The street was lined with beautiful trees. It was obvious that this was a perfect day with much that Mary could enjoy. But instead I saw a different picture. Mary was tricycling down the street on a lovely sunny day, blue skies above, surrounded by beautiful green trees and colorful blooming flowers, but something was missing. Mary was actually devoid of any emotion or any feeling. The beauty surrounding her went unnoticed. She was in a state of absolute apathy.

As I realized this, my power animal began to explain Mary's situation. "What you are seeing is Mary's coping mechanism for the lack of emotional support in her life. She has cut herself off from life so that she doesn't have to feel pain." He continued, "The cause of her disease is apathy, and the cure is passion. Mary is an example of what happens when another life form in the body has a stronger desire to live than the person in whom it resides. The illness takes over. It has more passion for life. Tell Mary the cause of her disease is apathy, and the cure is passion." He repeated this last phrase to me several times, indicating its serious and important nature.

The little girl riding the tricycle was about three years old. I asked her if she wanted to return to the adult Mary with me. She replied yes, instructing me that she would help Mary regain passion in her life. The three-year-old Mary showed herself as apathetic to reveal why she left, but when she left it was Mary's vitality she took with her. She was the vitality that Mary needed to continue living. Although retrieving this part of Mary's soul was the most significant part of the healing journey for her, my power animal instructed me to bring back more parts.

I continued my journey to find other pieces of Mary that would be helpful in her healing process. In the Upper World I discovered a thirteen-year-old girl who had entered womanhood with no role model to help her move gracefully into the next phase of her life. I also found a part of Mary that had left because of deep disappointment when a man she loved was forced out of her life by her controlling parents. Both of these parts of Mary wanted to return.

At this point I heard familiar words from my power animal: "That's enough for now. Leave me with these three parts." I have learned through time and practice never to ignore or question my power animal's instructions when doing healing work, for the Universe knows much better than I what is needed at the time.

I returned to my body carrying the three souls I had been instructed to bring back. I kept hearing the words echoing through my mind: "The cause is apathy; the cure is passion."

Maintaining concentration on the soul parts I had in my hands, I got up on my knees and blew the three parts into Mary's heart center and then, with Mary sitting up, into the crown of her head.

I welcomed Mary home, then recounted my journey, emphasizing that I didn't know whether the scene on the tricycle was metaphorical or literal. As I told her about the three-year-old, I saw a glimmer of life force spark in Mary's eyes.

Mary asked for more explanation of what I meant by saying that the cure for her is passion. *Passion* is a word that can easily be misunderstood, for aren't we a culture that has lost its passion for life? There are many good reasons for this—we all have our own stories of abuse—but regardless of the cause, the problem for Mary and many others is clear. How could I help Mary see the true meaning of passion?

I asked, "Mary, what kind of things are you passionate about? What gives you great joy to do? What would bring joy and meaning back into your life? Would it be fun to draw, or sculpt, or dance, or take walks? Use your imagination. In your wildest imagination, what could this passion possibly be?"

Mary was silent for a moment, then said she enjoyed taking walks. She didn't seem really enthused about this, but at least we had a starting place.

I have often seen people sabotage their visions because they pick unattainable goals that leave them feeling powerless, too paralyzed to take any action in life. So I believe that one of my roles is to teach the concept of taking "baby steps" in achieving goals.

With Mary the first step was to get her out walking. I asked her, "What are good times of the day for you to walk? Where do you like to walk? What is feasible for you right now? How can you make this a fun part of your everyday life?"

Mary answered all these questions. She seemed open to taking this step. And then she said something that threw me for a minute, "What happens if I cannot keep the three-year-old inside of me? I feel I need to let her go."

I listened to this question, remembering that the three-year-old was the part that was returning with the passion for life and also the life force that was missing in Mary. I believe that the rejection of this part was Mary's rejection of life. I realized—without judgment—that Mary was not willing to receive the healing.

We all have the right to make our own choices. Mary had made hers in an unconscious way, for she had no conscious awareness that she was rejecting life. I had total faith in Mary to make the right choice for herself.

I found myself thinking about the words I constantly repeat in my workshops, "Death is not a failure. Death is one way we heal."

I didn't want to project any of my thoughts onto Mary. I had done the work I needed to do on her behalf; Mary had to take responsibility for continuing that work. I told Mary she could send away any soul parts she wanted to. They had left her once before, thus they could leave again. The three-year-old could always be retrieved again at a later date when Mary was ready to have her home again.

I encouraged Mary to take walks and to continue to explore any activities that would bring passion or meaning back into her life. I wished her well.

After Mary left, I realized I had received an incredible teaching that would take a long time to digest. I kept hearing the words, "The lesson for Mary is to learn what happens when another life form in her body has more passion for life than she does." I had repeated this statement to Mary many times, hoping that on some level she would get the meaning. She died six months later, so perhaps she was ready for a different kind of transformation.

I wondered if I had received some clue to the meaning of illness. It is my experience that people in our culture have lost their passion for life. We have our share of life-threatening illnesses today. Diseases are forms of life (viruses, cancer cells, bacteria). Could it be that they are thriving because of our lack of passion for life?

But how can I help people renew passion in their lives? What question can I ask them to concentrate on after any healing work occurs? I sat back and looked out onto the piñon and juniper that surround my house. My attention drifted off into the trees. What is a beginning question for people?

I heard the words forming in my mind: "How do you want to use your creative energy, now that a healing has taken place and you are back in your body again? How do you want to use your creative energy to make something positive in your life instead of creating another illness, trauma, or drama?"

This was a start. I found myself becoming obsessed with the effort to help people move forward. This concept of creating the future that Isis had planted in my mind had me reeling with possibilities. I was fully aware that I was going to extremes with this particular issue, but because the scales are currently tipped toward focusing on the past, I felt that my extremist position might serve to create a bit of balance.

At this point in my work, I understand that the first step forward is for the client to be able to receive the healing. Once the healing is performed, the next step is for the client to start to look at life after illness, a process that involves two very crucial questions: What changes do I need to create in my life that will keep me healthy? How do I want to use my creative energy to make something positive in my life?

I like to give myself time to let ideas sink in at a very deep level. For me, this takes both time and silence. I am not a person who enjoys or benefits from overanalyzing ideas. I need to let new concepts become part of me in an inactive way, watering the ground and letting the moisture seep down into the roots where I can use it as needed over time.

The success of any healing is the ability of the client to receive the healing.

Trust your psyche to know how to heal.

In the end, we must take responsibility for our own healing process by making changes that are life-supportive.

Could one cause of illness be that other life forms, such as bacteria and viruses, have more passion to live than the person they are attacking? Is a person's passion for life one of the keys to healing?

Make your goals attainable so that you do not become overwhelmed and paralyzed by the immensity of your vision.

How do you want to use your creative energy to create a positive future for yourself?

Thought to ponder:

> *The Universe is not "out to get us." It is trying to heal us. It is safe to open to all that the Universe is trying to give us. It is safe to receive that love.*

EXERCISES

1. How might you foster the ability to receive in your own life? We receive through our senses; practice opening up some of your senses. Go outside. Find some form of nature to focus your

attention on. Pick one thing; it might be a plant, or a bird in the sky, or the sky itself, or a rock, or a tree, or an insect. Pick just one thing. Now stretch the muscles of your eyes wide to take in this object. Look at the color. Really look at it. Don't think about it. Receive it visually without analyzing what the object looks like.

Now look around you. You can remain outdoors or go back inside. Find some object that you can touch. Pick any object, animate or inanimate. Now let your hands feel this object. Allow yourself to soak up the feeling of the object. Is it soft, hard, cool, warm? What is the texture? Don't think about the process; allow it to happen. Allow yourself to receive the feeling.

Next find something that you can smell. Close your eyes, block out any intruding thoughts, and breathe in the smell. Allow it to happen.

Open up your ears to the sounds around you. You might want to concentrate on some natural sound rather than something mechanical. Take in the sound. Receive the sound.

There are other senses we could do this exercise with. There are invisible senses; there are the invisible senses we see and feel and hear and smell with. But for now you have done enough. By starting with the senses that are easier to access, we can begin to heighten our understanding of receptivity. Don't you feel more alive when you do this?

2. Before you go to bed, ask for a dream about how to strengthen your receptivity to life. Do this every night until you receive a dream that you can remember.

3. Have you been on a healing journey for some time? Have you done enough soul-searching about your past? Is it time for you to get on with your life? If your answer to this question is yes, allow yourself to brainstorm on the next question: What changes do I have to make in my life to keep myself emotionally and physically healthy?

Remember to limit your response to simple things that won't overwhelm you. If you become paralyzed by goals that are too lofty, you will not be taking a healing action toward yourself.

If you are trained in shamanic journeying, you might find it helpful to journey to one of your power animals or teachers to get help with this question.

I honor your courage in being willing to make a positive change in your life. And I hope you will honor yourself by being accepting and allowing yourself to work at your own pace. Know that by raising your awareness to these concepts you are working in your own behalf as well as in behalf of all life on the planet.

CHAPTER 3

"PSYCHIC LITTERING"

like coming to the surface
from a long, deep dive:
breath at last!
I am!

—*Linda Crane*

I have learned many of the important principles of life after healing through lessons from my teacher Isis. Two years ago I had a very surprising encounter that started me on a path of looking at the right use of thought energy—a crucial principle to understand in creating a positive present and future. This interaction was so powerful that I would like to share how my learning began.

"What was that thought?"

"What?" I asked, startled out of a deep space.

"What was that thought?" I heard again.

"Where is that voice coming from?" I wondered, as I sat in my backyard in a rocking chair looking out into space.

"It's me, Isis. What were you just thinking?"

I was shocked. Isis never appeared out of the blue like this. She must have something very important to talk about. I had been sitting and daydreaming when I heard her speak to me, so I went back into my thought process trying to remember what I had been daydreaming about and what might have caused Isis to appear like this. I realized I had been thinking about how angry I was about a recent interaction with a friend.

Isis repeated, "What was that thought? Where are you sending the energy behind the thought?"

"I was thinking about how angry I was at a friend of mine," I answered, "and I have no idea where that thought went."

"Well, maybe it is time for you to start thinking about this: Thoughts contain energy, and energy creates matter. It is time you become more responsible about how you use your energy."

"Isis, I think I understand the basis of what you are saying to me, but can you slow down and help me understand what you are getting at?"

I closed my eyes, but I could barely make out an image of Isis. This was one of those times when the words were more important than the vision. So I stopped struggling to see and settled in to listen to what Isis had to reveal to me.

"You teach in your workshops that spiritual intrusions that cause localized illness come from negative thought forms. It is time to slow down your own thought process and truly understand and take responsibility for the words that you teach. A statement like that has many ramifications for all life forms as well as for the earth. Your thoughts and words affect all life around you with the energy that is sent out."

I returned to my angry thoughts. I psychically attempted to retrieve the energy that I had just sent out.

"Now what are you going to do with that energy?" Isis asked. "You can't keep it, or else the energy from your anger can sit inside you and cause a spiritual intrusion."

"I'll give it to the earth. She will know what to do with it," I replied.

"I want you to contact the earth herself and ask her what she thinks of that solution."

I went into my house and got one of my drums. I took it outside to my chair and began to drum for myself.

The drumming allowed my soul to leave my body and go through my opening into the Lower World, which is a tree trunk. I quickly slid down the dark and windy earthen tunnel. I know how to speak to the earth; I have done it many times before in my journeys. I slid to a place deep inside the earth. I sat at a fire pit where the fire inside the earth answered questions that I put to her. I asked, "Will you take the feelings of anger that I have right now?"

The burning fire responded, "I am tired of having to clean up your energy. I don't want it anymore. There are too many people dumping all their energy on me. There was a time when I was willing to take the energy that was given to me and help change it. But that time is over. The people who used to ask for my help did it with care and respect. My life was sacred to them.

"Now there are billions of people who live on me. I am not looked upon as a sacred life form. My attention now is on all the millions of children who are starving, all the millions of people who are suffering. I am not willing to clean up your mess. Clean up your own mess."

This response shocked me. I had learned that one way to deal with feelings that needed to be expressed was to dig a hole in the earth and shout the problems and feelings into the hole; the earth would then take the energy for you. I felt thrown into crisis. I can't send my feelings out to someone else because I can cause an intrusion in him or her, yet I can't keep my feelings to myself because I can cause an intrusion inside myself. Now, I can't even send the energy to the earth because she doesn't want it.

"What am I supposed to do with this?" I cried out in desperation. I felt my anger had turned into a ball of nuclear waste that nobody wanted.

"Sandra, think!" Isis commanded.

I put out a call for help into the Universe.

"These are feelings that I hold. I have a right to have feelings. I have a right to express my feelings. Please take this anger and transform it into healing energy that can be used somewhere on the planet!"

"That is one way to deal with the energy," Isis responded. "That energy must be transmuted. The spirits have heard your call, and the work has been done."

I returned back up my tunnel from the center of the earth. I stopped drumming, opened my eyes, and snapped back to ordinary reality. I did not like where I had just been, but Isis's sudden appearance was obviously a message that I had been getting a very important lesson.

I was unaware of the process that was about to begin, however. Isis was not through with me yet. She was not simply planting a seed in me that I could just sit with and allow to grow. Instead, she wanted action. She wanted me to change my behavior. And she was going to stay close by constantly to make sure I did.

As I went about my life for the next few months, every time I had a negative thought, Isis would appear at my left shoulder and whisper into my ear, "What was that thought, and where did you just send it?"

I had no idea how many of my everyday thoughts were devoted to expressing some form of anger, frustration, disappointment, or worry. Eventually, with discipline, I could say with each negative thought that arose, "I need to express my feelings right now, but I do not want them to cause harm to another. I ask the Universe to take the energy behind these thoughts and transform them to healing energy that can be used somewhere on the planet."

What a practice this has become! Even though I realized that it was natural to have negative thoughts, I also recognized that I had to take some responsibility for the transmutation of these thoughts. I had always assumed that these thoughts were somehow magically taken care of.

All this was a new way of looking at the process of thought. Often, when I am trying to understand a process I am working with, I discuss it with my community of peers. Expressing ideas out loud this way usually brings me clarity.

So I decided to start talking about this concept of transforming negative energy at some of my workshops. As I had expected, there was a variety of responses from the people I spoke with. In one workshop David thought that what I had learned from Isis was very interesting and perhaps could be labeled "psychic littering." "Is it possible," he asked, "that the garbage problem on the planet today is a mirror of our own psychic littering?"

However, another workshop participant had a response that was not positive. She expressed her concern for the many incest survivors who were just learning how to get in touch with their feelings. Now I had suggested these feelings could hurt others. She felt that the process I was talking about was an advanced technique that had to be taught to others only with great care.

What she pointed out was true. I know with great certainty that Isis was not condemning me for my feelings. Feelings, for better or for worse, are part of the human experience. They are what make us human. To deny our feelings is to deny our own human experience. When we deny our feelings, we oppress our own life force and the right to express our own soul.

For me, the point of this lesson was learning how to transmute the energy behind the feelings instead of just dumping them into the psychic airwaves. The issue fascinated me. For one thing, Isis was constantly at my side reminding me of my current thoughts and asking me to stay present in the process of transmuting them. I decided that I needed to continue exploring this issue with other people.

In another workshop I decided to take this concept one step further. I had developed a very good relationship with the participants as we lived and worked together for a week. One focus of this particular workshop was on looking at the nature of ritual, the right use of ritual, and the retrieving of rituals to create change.

One of the exercises I had been teaching people for years was how to journey to descendants in the future for advice on current issues. Because a shamanic journey involves travel outside of time, we have the ability to journey forward as well as backward. If our thought forms are really littering the earth in a psychic way, then most likely this would become a problem for our descendants. And as time passed and consciousness evolved, solutions would be developed for this dilemma. In any event, I was sure that our descendants would have some enlightening reaction to this phenomenon, even if only to laugh at us.

I enlisted the assistance of anyone in the workshop group who was willing to journey into the future to retrieve guidance about psychic littering. (Because of the emotions that might arise from doing a journey such as this, I wanted to make it optional.) When the drumming began, I directed participants to put out a strong telepathic message to meet descendants who might have a message for us in the present about the concept of psychic littering and its cleanup. I reminded everyone that if any disturbing or "doom and gloom" messages were given, they were indications of hope for changing things. Why should the spirits give a warning message if there were no possibility for change? That would not be a healing intervention. We must remember that the Universe and the spirits are always trying to help heal.

As always, the spiritual guidance that came from the group's journeys was wonderfully varied, providing different aspects of this issue to explore. Common to all the journeys were that no "doom and gloom" messages were given and that all the information that came from the journeys was very gentle. Although the responses were varied, it appeared that people in the future had learned how to transmute energy and had developed methods to clean up the energy left behind by their ancestors. They felt no resentment about this; it was an issue of evolution, not of right or wrong.

Here are some examples of what people learned from their journeys.

Janie wrote:

Though I journeyed into the future, I found myself in a place familiar to me now—a beach on Lake Superior outside Grand Marais, Michigan. It looked very much as it does now and so did the people, except that both men and women wore their hair very, very short. A soft-spoken man who appeared to be in his forties acted as the spokesperson for the group of people on the beach. I told him I was seeking a ritual to transmute negative energy. He smiled and pointed to the west. The sky was streaked with color and clouds that looked as if they were on fire—a typical, spectacular Lake Superior sunset. He told me to visualize the moment the setting sun appears to make contact with the lake, when the surface of the water looks like molten gold as the two powerful forces merge. He said that if I pictured that moment, I would instinctively understand or feel that harmony was possible with the person about whom I'd had the negative thought, and I could then allow the energy to be transformed into liquid gold light. He told me the ritual could be done in an instant— literally, the blink of an eye—and that my signal to myself was to blink. My eye closing would show me the sunset and begin the transmutation, and my eye opening would finish it. All I needed was the split-second picture of sun touching water.

He suggested a different method to use when the negative thought originated from deep inside the heart and pertained to a loved one. He suggested that I "tingle my fingers." When I asked what that meant and how to do it, he replied that I should take a deep breath and feel my heart expanding, opening wide enough to forgive both the loved one and myself for the thought. He explained that the energy would be changed to love before it left my body, and I would feel it as a tingling in my fingertips as I exhaled.

They told me that they spend much time doing this kind of energy work and they meet regularly in groups to ritualize such transformations to deal with problems such as racism, warfare, boundaries, and hatred. Not everyone works with such groups, but many do. "It's rather like church work," he said.

Brooke's experience:

I journeyed to a circle of women beating a drum in the Middle World. I moved into the drum and then up onto a hilltop, where I was encircled by women in white robes beating a drum—in the future. The setting felt very ethereal, and the women had no hair. I asked for a ritual that I could do to transmute the energy from my negative thoughts so that it might be used for healing. I was told to "blink and say stardust." I thought this reminded me too much of Peter Pan and Tinkerbell, when we were supposed to clap and say, "I believe." Their answer was that it was much like that since what I was doing was changing my focus, through belief, and willing the negativity to become again the basic stuff of life, what we are all made up of: stardust. Through my own willingness to take action and transmute the energy in that moment of intention, focus, and belief, I act on my power to change the world.

For Teddy this was a tough question:

I went to the Upper World. Wind took me to a young woman with long, dark hair and a lovely light-beaded dress.

She thought a long time and then suggested I squeeze a crystal in my pocket or mentally send negative energy to a crystal.

The crystals should be cleaned weekly by setting them out in direct sunlight. The sun's energy would dissipate any negativity.

I thanked her and said that seemed like a lot of work.

She said it was one of the more constructive ways of dealing with negative energy.

I gave her a kiss and a flower and thanked her again.

Nancy relates:

I journeyed to my descendants for a ritual on the transmutation of energy. My descendants were farmers. The man and the woman were delighted to see me and walked with me about their farm, showing me the plants that grew.

The man said he took his negative thoughts, anything that he disliked or hated, such as his job, another person, or a situation, and gave it love, surrounding the negative thought or object in red, pink, or the color of the inside of his body. Then he dug a hole in the earth and gave the energy to the earth, putting his love into the hole with it.

The woman likened this process to composting. When she was in a negative situation, the method she used was like planting corn. She meditated on the situation and gave the negative thoughts to the garbage; she then blessed it with her love and gratitude and buried the garbage and blessing in the garden around the corn or whatever plants she had in the garden.

Almost one year later Nancy decided to do another journey on this topic, this time consulting with her teacher in nonordinary reality. She wrote:

My teacher said that to know the feelings associated with creative energy was extremely important, for the river of life begins with this energy. To begin anything, or change anything, I was to begin from a place of balance, harmony, and love of self. My teacher gave me a special self-love process in which I sent love to

all of me—to my body, to my emotional self, to my intellectual
self, and to my spiritual self. I am to express love and approval
to each self every morning. And whenever I am to begin a new
project, or I am in a difficult situation, I am to stay centered and
come to the project or situation from this place of self-love.

My teacher stated that this is a most powerful place to come
from, as the energy that I am and the energy I send out are one
and the same. If I am negative, I will send out negative energy,
and the results will be more negative, and if I am centered
and have positive energy about myself, then I will send out posi-
tive energy, and the result will have a greater chance of being
positive.

This to date has proved to be very successful.

Everyone in the workshop agreed that when we look at the behavior of human beings before our time, there can be no evaluation of right and wrong. It is so important not to view the past from a place of judgment but to acknowledge that this is what the collective was working on at the time. This nonjudgmental way of looking at the past gives us the freedom to change.

I had anticipated one response that was still unspoken. I hoped that someone had got a different piece of the puzzle. There are many ways to look at any particular issue; likewise, there are many individual pieces that make up one complete puzzle. Finally, Jan, a participant who had been silent during the conversation on psychic energy, piped up. "I had a very different journey than the rest of you. The descendant I met said that energy was just energy, not negative or positive. Energy just was and could always be seen as neutral and used as such."

This was the response I was waiting for. I did understand that concept. The spiritual response to energy is neutral. It is not good or bad, it just is. Another whole practice could be devoted to this concept. But the two concepts are not as contradictory as they seem. Yes, from a very esoteric view, energy is neutral. Yes, if you know what you are doing, you can use all the energy that is flying around the airwaves to help you.

But what I was being asked to look at was different. How was I behaving on the level of energy? I was not being asked to look at this issue out of guilt; guilt has no place in any spiritual practice. In fact, guilt should have no place in most of our lives, because it causes illness. Isis wanted me to take responsibility for how I was using my energy and asked me to be more conscious of the effect of my energy on myself, on others, and on the planet. Although I understood the concept of neutral energy, I also realized that Isis had given me an incredible gift by calling my attention to this issue.

I believe that indigenous people knew the effect of energy on others. Long before modern technology created bombs that could be dropped, people practiced psychic warfare, in which harmful spiritual intrusions were sent to enemies or souls were stolen to take personal power and life force from other people.

The concept of psychic warfare is probably shocking to people in modern times. But don't we still behave in the same way today, even though on an unconscious level? Isn't it more dangerous that this behavior stays at an unconscious level rather than at a conscious level, where there are "rules" to be followed? Isn't it time that we take responsibility for looking at how our thoughts and energy affect ourselves, people around us, and the planet?

I have always been extremely sensitive to energy. Once, I actually realized that the language of energy is my first language, instead of English. I struggled to learn English, and I began to speak at a very late age. I always thought that everyone just naturally knew what I was trying to communicate. When I started counseling people and teaching workshops, I was shocked to find out that people didn't automatically understand what I was saying and that I had to learn to be a clear communicator. Now Isis was asking me to go back to this form of invisible communication, dissect and understand it, and become more proficient in it.

Now I was being asked to teach people about invisible language, about how to become more aware of their communication in energy terms, just as in many forms of therapy and in business people are taught about verbal communication skills. For isn't it true that we all communicate without words every waking second of our lives?

To be able to share this information with others, I had to begin with myself. So I found myself day-to-day, minute-to-minute, listening to what I was putting out to the world through silent language. I had to keep up the discipline of transforming the energy behind my thoughts into healing energy. I learned how important it was to be honest about my feelings and to express them for my own health and welfare. I learned how this could be of benefit to all. Isis and the Universe were with me at all times during my learning, and I knew I had all the support and guidance and love that I needed for this teaching.

As the months turned and life kept flowing, I was very much aware of an energy shift inside myself. On a positive level, I was feeling good about the discipline of watching my thoughts; it seemed to become an automatic process for me that did not require a significant amount of attention. On the problematic side, I felt hypersensitive to the energy around me. I felt uncomfortable in large groups of people and in populated cities. Sometimes it seemed that it really was "a jungle out there." Thought forms were flying around everywhere. Imagine all the energy that comes from the frustration, anger, and despair of people living in overcrowded cities! Imagine being able to see and feel and truly experience this!

This is a serious problem for me. But through the years of working with my helping spirits, I have learned to laugh at myself and the human experience. Humor keeps us centered and in balance, no matter how "sick" the humor seems. My power animal loves to give me comical images to encourage me to laugh. He has also taught me how to use laughter as a form of protection. I find that energy changes when I can laugh at it. So although my new discipline was a serious one, I also learned how to diffuse any harmful effects by laughing.

There are other forms of protection I use. The first and most important principle of protection is not allowing myself to fall prey to irrational fear. Fear creates an opening for harmful energy to enter. I had learned in years prior that the only way for harmful energy to truly have an effect on me was to allow it to. I am quite clear about boundaries and about my ability to control what flows in and out of me, so I have to participate actively in the experience of allowing harm to enter.

The first step for me was to learn how to become aware of the energy around me. What was the invisible language that was being communicated to me when I was out in the world and in the presence of others? By becoming aware of my surroundings, I could choose what I wanted to open to and what I needed to shut off. When I felt a need to close down (which actually wasn't very often) I used a method that was taught to me by a Chumash medicine woman years before. I would experience myself by either seeing or feeling a translucent blue egg around me. When I was inside the egg, I could interact fully with those around me, but nothing outside my energy field could get in. And I always could telepathically call my power animal to me, asking for his assistance in providing protection.

Every year I use the blue egg less often. What I have learned is that I am not a fragile person. I can say no to energy that is coming to me. I also can choose to be permeable to the energy coming to me. With the help of the Universe, I can always transmute and use any energy.

I would soon have the experience of trying to teach this material to individuals learning how to set boundaries in their own lives as well as to people in the helping professions who needed to understand the effects of the energy they take on while working with others.

It is part of the human experience to have a range of thoughts and feelings.

Thoughts are forms that create energy that affects ourselves, other people, and all of life.

From an esoteric perspective, all energy is neutral and is always usable in whatever form it takes.

We can protect ourselves from negative energy by maintaining our center at all times and not moving into a place of fear. We can also surround ourselves with a translucent blue egg or psychically call on our helping spirits for protection.

We can choose to accept or resist any energy that is around us.

Thought to ponder:

> *We can learn how to transform the energy behind our thoughts. Can similar principles be used to transmute pollution and toxins in our environment?*

EXERCISES

1. Observe your thoughts. Do not judge these thoughts, just observe them. No one can invalidate your feelings or thoughts.

2. If you choose, ask any thought forms of a problematic nature to be transformed to healing energy that can be used somewhere on the planet.

3. In any public place, see and feel if you can become aware of the energy around you. Again, try to be nonjudgmental.

4. If you need help creating boundaries against the energy around you, try putting yourself into a translucent blue egg or telepathically calling your helping spirits to you.

CHAPTER 4

SETTING
BOUNDARIES

Bruce, a psychologist, came to me complaining of stomach problems and a serious lack of energy. After we talked for a while, I explained to him that I needed to journey to my power animal to find the spiritual diagnosis of his problem. I would journey down to my power place in the Lower World and briefly ask my power animal for an explanation of the problem and the appropriate shamanic method of healing.

My power place is very lush. A lagoon with a waterfall is surrounded by tall pine trees. The ground around it is covered with pine needles. I feel nurtured by the Universe when I come to this place and sit on the soft ground to meet with my power animal. The smell of pine reminds me of my connection to nature and how its beauty feeds all of my senses. The smell, the touch, the colors there—I just love it.

My power animal was waiting for me, and we sat down and began our conversation. He telepathically explained Bruce's problem. Bruce is an empath, which is one reason that he is such a wonderful psychologist: he can experience his clients' feelings. But Bruce has not learned how to set boundaries between himself and his clients. He doesn't know how to let go of the feelings that he has taken on during his work, and he also doesn't know how not to give away his energy to his clients.

The sadness, anger, and frustration Bruce has taken on from his clients, my power animal told me, have formed a spiritual intrusion in his stomach, causing a blockage that makes it difficult for him to digest his food. He also said that Bruce has unconsciously given up his soul, his life force, to his clients, and that has caused his severe loss of energy. The blockage in his stomach also contributes to this condition.

My power animal instructed me to return to Bruce, speak to him about this message, and perform a shamanic extraction to remove the intrusion and blockage in his stomach. I was also to do a soul retrieval to gather the pieces of Bruce that he had given away to his clients, thus returning his life force and energy to him. My animal told me to teach Bruce about what happens on the energy level when he sees clients, and how he can take care of himself and prevent these problems from recurring.

Using the drumbeat to leave the Lower World, I retraced my steps into my room. I stopped drumming and opened my eyes to see Bruce anxiously awaiting any information that I had for him. I repeated everything that my power animal had said.

Bruce completely understood the information I gave him. "I know I take on clients' pain, and I know I give pieces of myself away. What I didn't know was what this was doing to me on a physical level. What happens next?"

I explained to Bruce that I was going to perform a shamanic extraction to remove the energy block in his stomach, and then I would retrieve his soul to bring back his vital energy. After the work was completed, the next step would be to help Bruce understand how to change his behavior during his sessions with clients. How does one learn not to repeat the same patterns?

First I helped Bruce look at how to let go of his clients' pain. I began by telling him how I work with this issue myself, because I too am a very empathetic person. I use the pain I feel as information to understand what another person's experience is. But once I have received the information, I say to myself, "This is not my pain, and I can let it go."

When we become enmeshed in another person's pain or energy, we can lose sight of whose energy it is we are experiencing. One exercise I recommend is to simply look inside yourself and ask, "Is this my pain? Is this my experience, or does this belong to someone else?" Pay attention to the first thought that comes up, do not edit, and go with that response. Once it is clear that this is not your pain, silently ask yourself to let it go. If it *is* your pain or your experience, then you can process it through doing your own work.

Bruce liked the idea of checking in at various times of the day to make sure he was not carrying someone else's pain. But he still felt he needed something more to facilitate the process of letting go.

I often use ritual to help let go of pain. I talked to Bruce about the nature of ritual and told him how powerful I thought it would be if he could take the pain he was holding and transmute it to healing energy. I suggested he shut his eyes, relax, and take a few deep breaths to center himself. Then I asked him if from this centered place he could think of a ritual of release that would feel good to do. With eyes still closed, he described an image of himself holding a glass of water, then releasing any energy that is not his through his hand into the water. As he holds the glass he asks for the water to change the energy to healing energy. Next he sets the glass of water outside, allowing the sun to release the healing energy into the sky. Finally, he waters the ground. At this point Bruce opened his eyes, which were bright and seemed to be laughing. He really liked the ritual he had created.

The power of ritual is intention, and the ritual will work for Bruce as long as he is clear about why he is doing it. He said he would do that ritual on a regular basis. My feeling was that after Bruce has been acting on this learning by doing the ritual with the water, he eventually will get to the point where he won't need this tool anymore. As he evolves, he will begin transforming the energy naturally on his own. But this ritual was a wonderful beginning.

We moved to the next issue: how to stop the process of giving his soul away in his client sessions. We also had to make sure that no one was stealing his soul in the sessions. Neither is uncommon in any helping profession; a practitioner may fall prey to soul stealing or may give away a piece of his or her own soul in an attempt to help another person.

As I discuss in my earlier book, *Soul Retrieval: Mending the Fragmented Self,* we do not help another person by giving away our soul. Other people cannot use our vitality, power, light, or energy for themselves. In giving up a soul part, we often burden others with unusable energy. This concept is a very important one for us to understand in our lives after healing. We must learn how to keep our energy for ourselves and not try to take the energy of another. We must become self-contained on the energy level.

I explained to Bruce, "The first step is to raise your awareness of what is happening to you on an energy level. Start by observing when in your sessions you become unusually tired. At this point, note whether you are giving your soul away or whether someone else is attempting to steal it. Just identify the situation. Do not judge it. From where in your body does your soul leave when this happens?"

Bruce needed some help with this concept. I suggested he close his eyes and just breathe for a while. I asked him to search his mind for a time when he had felt himself getting suddenly exhausted in his work. He remembered a recent session. As he pictured that session, I asked him to watch himself and his client on an energy level to identify the energy communication that was taking place. He felt an invisible force leaving from his solar plexus. Was he giving it up to his client, or was his client pulling in that energy? Bruce said he understood the difference and that here he was giving up his energy because he wanted to help. But he couldn't sense how that energy was helping. It seemed to be stuck on his client. When I asked him if he could pull it back in, he said he could.

Bruce wanted to look at one more session. I encouraged him to take his time and to talk out loud as much as possible so I could track him and help him see what was happening. He suspected that one of his clients was taking his energy. I led him by saying, "See yourself in session with this client. Watch the energy in the room. Watch when the energy begins to shift. Notice when you feel your energy leaving your body." He felt a tug on his solar plexus and could see his client tugging on his energy. I asked him to envision himself at this moment in a translucent blue egg, repeating silently to himself, "I refuse to give up my soul to you." He experienced the image and said the words to himself. "What a difference that makes!" he said.

I instructed Bruce to keep breathing until he felt ready to open his eyes and bring his awareness back into the room so we could discuss his experience. He found that he could actually see the energy in the room. I explained to him that it didn't take any special gift to do that. We all have the capability; it just takes a shift in perception. It takes becoming aware of what is happening to one's energy, declaring an intention not to release that energy, and setting a boundary around oneself when appropriate. Bruce agreed that he could do this, even during his client sessions.

We had done a tremendous amount of work in our session, but I wanted Bruce to look at one more issue. I asked him to honor his process and where he was right now. Could he look at one more issue?

He wanted to continue but needed a short break. So we went outside into my garden. I was becoming a little sloppy with my garden tending. The weeds were looking healthy, and my vegetables were starting to go to seed. I was disappointed that I was not taking better care of my garden, yet there was an incredible beauty to the wildness apparent in not trying to control what was growing. This beauty in letting things grow out of control can be a big lesson for someone with many control issues.

We sat in the garden soaking up the sun for a while. Bruce realized that he forgets to take breaks in his work with people. He recognized that it is difficult to maintain concentration in his sessions if he just goes from one session to another without a way to center himself between clients. He said he will take a new look at how he schedules people.

I encouraged him in this way of thinking. Another aspect of life after healing is learning how to take care of yourself and honor your needs. Bruce was learning about how he could stay healthy after our initial work together. After some garden talk and taking in the sun, Bruce decided it was time to go back to work.

Back in my office, I explained the final issue I wanted him to look at that day. "How do you let negative thought forms into your body? I want you to learn how not to do this so you don't have to create another block or illness in your body."

I asked Bruce to take a few deep breaths, close his eyes, and find his center. I asked him to search his mind for a session in which one of his clients was releasing anger. He said that was easy to do; he just had to find one to focus on. When he was ready, I instructed him to watch himself and his client at the point just before the anger work began. Then I asked him to watch what happened as his client began to release. He said, "I am watching myself being punched in the stomach by an invisible force."

I asked Bruce to back up the scene in his mind again. I suggested that as his client began to express emotion, he put himself into the translucent blue egg, and that as his client expressed

energy, he ask for that energy to be transformed into healing energy.

In doing this, Bruce realized that he could avoid taking on his clients' feelings and allowing them to make him ill. By setting boundaries to protect himself and by becoming aware of which feelings belong to him and which ones belong to others, Bruce can maintain his own physical integrity and health.

Bruce stayed in touch with me for the next few months. His work with setting boundaries and not allowing himself to take on others' pain or lose his soul in his sessions brought him back to the state of health he was seeking. His energy returned, and he didn't have any more stomach problems. He also felt that his sessions had become much more powerful: His clients seemed to be getting stronger without his having to lose any parts of himself in the process.

I firmly believe that people who are involved in the helping professions need to learn about what happens on an energy level between them and their clients. Here I refer to people in the medical profession as well as those involved with counseling and psychology. It is not uncommon for someone who spends time in a hospital room to feel totally exhausted and drained afterward. Likewise, it is not unusual for people who are in the helping professions to feel "sucked dry" after a day at work. "Burnout" is a major problem. People need to learn how to prevent the illness that is caused by taking on the negative thought forms that abound in any situation of emotional or physical illness. If they understood what was happening on an energy level as well as how to set boundaries on a spiritual level in sessions with clients and patients, much of the burnout could be prevented.

Helping professionals are not the only people who need to learn how to set boundaries. All of us who choose to be in relationships with others also have this work to do.

Nancy came to see me complaining of a long stream of emotionally abusive and unhealthy relationships. She had heard about my work, and she hoped to get some relief from the unhealthy pattern she had set up for herself. Through shamanic journeying I was able to see where this pattern had started and to bring back the soul parts that she needed in order to clear the slate. Once the original trauma that began the pattern is resolved by the return of the dissociated parts, the person has the freedom to choose a different way of life.

Nancy had lost her soul at an early age when her mother judged her as unworthy. There was nothing Nancy could do without being yelled at. Because she was very young at the time, Nancy didn't understand that her mother was treating her this way because she was so frustrated with her own life. All Nancy knew was that she couldn't do anything right.

Taking this on as a core belief, Nancy went through life getting that belief mirrored back to her. Thus began the pattern that all the men she attracted into her life judged her. Sure enough, she could never do anything right in these relationships either. The men in her life were abusive toward her.

Nancy wanted to know what she had to do to change her life now that her lost soul parts were intact inside her again. I knew from my past experience with doing soul retrievals that afterward people naturally begin to set boundaries in their relationships. It makes sense. Once one is "back home" and whole, the understanding of who one is and what one needs becomes more clear. Awareness of one's own identity is heightened.

But I wanted to give Nancy the chance to allow her posthealing process to be more active and conscious, because this was what she requested. I asked Nancy if she had any interest in learning how to journey to the soul parts I returned to her and to her own power animal, who might have some guidance for her. Nancy said she would love to learn to journey. I told her that first I wanted to let the soul parts settle into her body for a few days. We set up another appointment so we could continue our work together.

When Nancy returned for our next session, I explained the process of journeying. I told her that this work would give her access to her own helping spirits so she could answer questions in her life, thus giving her back the power to make decisions that would be beneficial for her. I told her that we would start by learning how to go to the Lower World to find out who her own power animal was at this time. The Lower World is just one of the territories in nonordinary reality and seems to be a good place to start people in their work with shamanic journeying.

I drummed for Nancy to provide the path out of and back to her body. I gave her the usual instructions for entering the Lower World: I asked her to think about an opening in the earth that she could enter—someplace that she had actually seen before. In this way she would know whether she was in ordinary or nonordinary reality. I emphasized that shamanism is a discipline in which it is very important to know what world one is in at all times. So when one's starting place is in ordinary reality, it is very clear at both the start and the finish of the journey which reality one is in.

Nancy asked me if there was anything to fear in the Lower World. I answered that she had full control of her actions in a journey and so if something frightened her, she could always confront her fear, move away from it, or come back at any time.

To help her understand, I told her how Stephen, a good friend of mine, distinguishes between dreaming, daydreaming, and a shamanic journey. He explains that unless one has studied lucid dreaming, one has no control over what is happening in a dream. Thus, in a nightmare, the dreamer just has to pray to wake up soon. In a daydream, however, the daydreamer controls everything: who she meets, what she says, what the other person in the daydream does and says—everything is made up. Similarly, in a shamanic journey, the person has control over what she does. She can move to the left or to the right. She can move closer to an animal or another being waiting for her, or she can move away from it. But she cannot control what the animal or being does or says.

This explanation made perfect sense to Nancy. I asked her to lie down and put a bandana over her eyes to block out the light, for in shamanism we see in the dark. I also explained to Nancy that the words *shamanic seeing* didn't necessarily mean visual seeing, and I instructed her to open up to all the senses she might use to access information. As soon as she heard the drumming, she was to enter the opening into the earth she had chosen, go down her tunnel, and put out a very strong telepathic message for her power animal to be waiting for her on the other side.

She was to ask her power animal a simple yes-or-no question to see how it communicated with her. Some power animals communicate telepathically, some show symbols as an answer, and others will take the journeyer somewhere to show the answer. Once Nancy understood her animal's form of communication, she could ask it any question she chose.

We had already talked about trying to get guidance on changing her relationships, so she knew what kind of information she was seeking. Because this was Nancy's first journey, I didn't know how much she would be able to do. Some people only get into the tunnel on the first journey; first journeys for other people could be made into major motion pictures. The outcome involves the person's own natural timing with this work and has nothing to do with the issue of power.

Nancy's first journey was a powerful experience for her. This was how she described her journey when she reported back to me:

> I entered the earth through a cave at Carlsbad Caverns. I found myself running very fast through the tunnel. I kept hearing myself saying that I couldn't do this right. I hated hearing these words. But I have heard them so many times from my mother and from the men in my life that I have lost confidence in myself. I felt uncomfortable with the performance pressure as I ran

down the tunnel. But I followed your instructions and kept calling for my power animal to appear. Suddenly I saw a light at the end of the tunnel. I followed it out. Right there was a huge female tiger waiting for me. She was so beautiful. I could not believe how bright her eyes were. I just burst into tears when I saw her because she greeted me by saying, "I love you." I don't know how I heard those words, for her lips did not move. But I heard them very clearly. I not only heard those words, but I felt them in my body. I realized that I had never experienced that kind of love before. She gazed into my eyes, and I just couldn't stop crying. She sat with me. I began to stroke her fur. I could feel the wetness and softness of her fur.

I asked her if she would take me to the soul parts that Sandy had returned to me. She nodded and telepathically instructed me to hop on her back. We rode to this grassy place on the earth where we were surrounded by mountains and a very clear blue sky. There was a blanket on the ground waiting for us and—can you imagine!—there was a picnic basket there too. As we rode closer, I could see three young people on the blanket. They were me. They were the three parts that Sandy had brought back. The younger one, the first part that Sandy retrieved, ran up to us. The tiger licked her face, and she giggled. I got off the tiger and picked her up. You were right. Even though I knew that the parts were inside of me, in nonordinary reality it was possible to meet them as separate entities. I tried to remember what you had instructed me to ask them if I met them. I remembered the instructions to get a dialogue going. The youngest part, the five-year-old, told me how awful it was to always have Mom yelling at her. She was so small, and the words seemed overwhelming and harsh; she felt so scared and fragile. Who would protect her? I realized at this point that I always feel fragile. I always feel that everyone around me is much stronger and bigger. I wondered if that was a result of the trauma the five-year-old experienced. The other soul parts, which were much older,

left because of different relationships I was in. They did not ap-
pear to be as fragile as the five-year-old part. But all three had
something to say to me. The bottom line is that they wouldn't
come back to experience again the abuse that caused them to
leave in the first place. They wanted me to choose the people in
my life much more carefully, and they assured me they would be
there to help.

We ate together and played with the tiger. I had never felt
such love and strength. The tiger assured me that she was there
for me, to just call on her and please come back to see her again.
She had a lot to teach me. She told me that I needed to be strong
with people and to not give my power away in relationships. I
needed to stand up for myself and say when I didn't like how I
was being treated.

As she was giving me those instructions, I heard you signal-
ing me back with a change in the drumbeat. I remembered your
instructions to thank my animal and say good-bye to it as I was
leaving. So I thanked my tiger and said good-bye. I kissed all my
soul parts, and as I did that, we became one again. I turned
around and retraced my steps up the tunnel and out of the open-
ing of the cave in Carlsbad Caverns.

When you finished with the last of the return drumbeats, I
took a deep breath. I knew I was back in the room, but I didn't
want to open my eyes yet. I wanted some time to myself. It was
so great when you said to just be silent and with myself for a
while. I swore you were reading my mind.

When Nancy finally felt ready to talk, she took off the bandana and sat up. After she recounted her journey, I congratulated
her on her experience. She had done a lot for a first journey. But
Nancy was committed and ready to change. She came to me
knowing her life was not working, and she wanted to make it
work.

Nancy felt that when she was actually face-to-face with the soul parts that I had returned for her, she understood on a very deep level how she had been giving away her power and compromising herself in her relationships. Seeing the faces that belonged to some traumatic relationships reminded her of how she had "numbed out" to being mistreated. At this point she knew she could never do it again, nor could she remain in contact with people who were not willing to see that she was a good person who deserved love.

Because most of the work I do is shamanic healing, it is the reference point I use when I talk about the process that comes after any healing work. In shamanism we are looking at the spiritual aspect of illness. I know that it is also possible to come to a place of wholeness when one embarks on a path of medical and/or psychological treatment. All these paths lead to the same place: trying to be a whole person. A person like Nancy, who knows herself and no longer needs to see everyone she comes into contact with as a projection of the past, is in the process of becoming a whole person.

I am convinced that setting boundaries, knowing oneself, and having a strong identity are the keys to life after healing; from them flows the creation of a positive future for oneself—and the planet.

Developing a strong identity means no longer being enmeshed emotionally and psychically with others, and it seems to be a theme in all forms of emotional and spiritual healing. My book *Soul Retrieval* contains a chapter on soul stealing. Like the sending of negative thought forms, soul stealing is a behavior that we as a society practice unconsciously. One aspect of realizing how enmeshed we are with other people involves our becoming whole and seeing ourselves as separate individuals; however, that is only half the process. We must also see who we are holding onto on a psychic level. This also affects our ability to set boundaries. We can feel whole, but as long as we are holding onto another person on an energy level, we are not free to experience ourselves as a separate entity. I strongly suggest that each person finish the process of healing by releasing any souls he or she might have stolen.

Please be compassionate with yourself as you go through this process. Soul stealing is learned behavior, just as giving up one's soul is learned behavior. The point here is not for us to blame each other, but to evolve as a society, to get beyond re-creating past illness.

Here are some other examples of the experience of setting boundaries and how that can create positive change in a person's life.

> Since the five-day workshop I did, much has changed and integrated in my life. I received four soul essences back during my soul retrieval. One was my four-year-old abused child; two essences were from my deceased husband and my sister; and the fourth was my female warrior. Quite a handful, to say the least! While the stories are intertwined in relationship to life-learning, it is the tale of the female warrior that I wish to tell.
>
> According to my shamanic practitioner, my female warrior left because I had given away my power to men with whom I work and have intimate relationships. This statement immediately rang true to me.
>
> I saw the men in my life as above me, in positions of authority. Through the years I kept them there. As I did so, my strong feminine force took a vacation. She left in disgust or just plain outrage.
>
> After she returned, I felt so big. It was as if I had grown twelve feet tall. She promised to come back, after much negotiation, and said she would stay as long as I worked to honor this aspect of my being. A lot of her leaving had to do with the

abused child—not having safe boundaries and being invaded spiritually, emotionally, mentally. My abuse came from my grandmother, who chained me to a telephone pole for many years of my early childhood and ignored me as an intrusion in her life. She was my primary care-giver between the ages of six months and seven years. The formative years were quite terrible for me. I have been in therapy for two years now. Slowly I am coming to memory, and as I am working, I see the pattern of habitually giving myself away. Psychic attacks are the most horrific form of giving up pieces of myself. I have also been studying shamanism and holistic healing for many years. This has been through a personal unconscious drive for my own healing. Even before I started to unravel the cords, I knew deep down that I was missing essences of self. My journey has brought me to an understanding of a psychotic split that I lived through. For many years I have been ambivalent about even staying upon the earth for the rest of the journey. Since my soul retrieval, this ambivalence has changed dramatically. I choose life now in a conscious, joyous manner full of respect.

When I stepped back into my life after the seminar was over, I noticed that a shift had occurred. It isn't that I tried for change or tried to act differently; I just felt differently about many of the ongoing issues in my life.

My daughter is a good example of this "different" way of feeling or acting. She and I have been enmeshed for years. It is difficult for me to set boundaries with her and even sometimes to differentiate where I stop and she begins. After the seminar I saw her differently. She is really her own person, and that is the way it should be. Rather than become angry when she pushes against the limits that I set, I now just tell her what I expect and follow it with logical consequences. I remain calm, firm, and loving. Before, as she argued with me, I would get so angry that I would completely lose my temper and yell. Then instead of

being able to enforce limits, I would be so sorry for the bad way
I acted that the original issue was lost. This doesn't happen any-
more. I am also able to listen better to what she tells me, and
we have shared some very important, deep discussions about rel-
evant subjects. It is OK with me now for her to be a different,
separate person from me.

The seminar leader said changes in ourselves would not be so
evident to us but that those around us would notice and give
feedback on our changed behavior. My mother noticed a change.
I am now able to let her just be who she is, and sometimes that
is drunk and abusive. I don't stay around for the abuse, but I
don't have to get so upset anymore when she forsakes me, her
daughter, for her booze.

The person who has been the most supportive of and the
most verbal about the changes he sees in me is my ex-husband.
He says that I am so different and easy to deal with. He likes
me much better now. Could it be that being scared crippled me
here also? I am not sure. One change I made after the seminar
was to clearly and completely break off my relationship with my
lover. I had been trying to accomplish this feat for years. Each
time I would be about to end our relationship for good, some-
thing would happen—either my car would break or something
else would happen that I felt I couldn't handle alone. This time,
with my car broken down in my driveway, I was able to finally
be a whole person, stand up and do it! It was tremendously em-
powering! I am finally able to say that I, Mary Jeanne, tolerate
no more abuse in my life!

I wasn't prepared for the emotional impact following the cere-
mony. And I didn't need to do anything but let it happen! . . .
Ever since the soul retrieval, I have not felt that awful feeling that
something is wrong with me, no matter what the circumstances.
I no longer feel that when something doesn't feel right, or any-
thing seems wrong within my area of perception, that somehow

. . . it's my fault. And if thoughts, old thoughts, of blame, responsibility, negativity pass through my mind, I have some control over them. They don't adhere. There isn't a hole inside.

I never could understand that hole, or really see it, or explain it. It kept changing. I denied it was there for years and couldn't understand what others were talking about. I know it was dark and cold, fathomless and full of tears, which kept draining off so the lake full of them got smaller but never went away—and felt as if it never would. I always felt ashamed to admit I had this "lack," because I thought I shouldn't, and it was my fault that I did. Somehow if I could just do something different, or be different, it would go away.

Well, I think it's gone. I feel solid inside. I feel warm. Although I feel sad at times, the sadness doesn't hook into some bottomless well. It just passes through. And all the work I've done on changing my thought process—when the new ways of thinking pass across my mind, they can cling and stay. There's something that tells them it's OK to stay, that I'm not a hopeless place for them to be. (And I'm not hopeless when they don't stay!)

Most important, I think, is that I no longer abuse myself in my mind, at least that I'm aware of. I can ease up on myself. I can stop when I say something that doesn't feel good. I can tell myself it's OK to feel good and believe it! Feeling good or not feeling good is a signal that I can act on for the first time—and I can trust it. I know at my very core that what I feel is me, and it's OK, that there really is a me in there. When I think or feel something, it comes directly from me. Everything doesn't go through a filter system of "shoulds" and "shouldn'ts" that make it no longer mine. I think perhaps the wounds from verbal abuse that kept rampaging forever and insidiously through my head and kept me bleeding are healed at last. The words I've used to myself so constantly, and so much more destructively than I'd known, don't have to be beaten back, an effort that wore me out and that I couldn't keep up for long. They just aren't there at all!

I can hardly believe it! Even when I say mildly questioning things to myself, I can catch and stop them before they get out of control.

As a helping professional, one must learn to separate and protect oneself from a client's or patient's issues.

One must learn how to release and let go of any intense feelings shared in a session.

We must not only raise our awareness to any shifts in physical and emotional energy when we are in the presence of another person but also choose both not to allow our essence to be taken and not to steal someone else's soul.

We can choose life-supportive relationships in our lives.

The key to creating a positive future is to learn who you are so you know the difference between what is your vision and voice and what belongs to other people around you.

Thought to ponder:

What we give, we receive.

EXERCISES

1. Who are you enmeshed with? Can you separate who you are as a person from who they are? How do you project your issues onto them? How do they project their issues onto you?

2. Is there anyone in your life that you have an "unnatural" connection with, a person you feel is not in your life by mutual agreement?

Create a ritual to break the unnatural part of your connection—gather your soul back from that person or release that person's soul back to him or her. As you do this, notice how your relationships change with everyone around you.

3. Write down the name of every person you need to learn how to say no to. How is this a yes to yourself?

CHAPTER 5

USING YOUR CREATIVE ENERGY

It takes an amazing amount of energy to maintain any kind of illness, whether it be emotional, physical, or spiritual. To stay in a place of illness goes against nature, and it takes a lot of energy to keep going against the flow. I remember when I was dealing with chronic depression how exhausted I was, trying to keep my energy from moving.

After a person has been engaged in a healing process, a tremendous amount of energy is freed up. At this point one can choose to use that free energy to create another illness, trauma, or drama; or one can choose to use that freed-up energy to create positive life situations. The first step is to decide which way to go. Illness can become a habit, and the first step to breaking a habit, I believe, is making a conscious decision to do so.

I remember after my own healing process had taken place and I was more awake to my past patterns of behavior, I was horrified to see how I constantly chose pain over joy in my life. Being in a very different state after healing, I was very clear that I didn't want to make that choice anymore. I couldn't see any reason to live a life full of pain. I remember at that moment making a clear promise and statement to myself: If I was going to be here, living and functioning on this planet, then I was going to be more conscious about how I used my energy. I was going to use all the energy I had put into being ill and depressed to create a joyful and meaningful life for myself. This was the first step. Once I made a clear and conscious decision in this matter, I found that my life changed drastically. That was probably the most important decision I have ever made.

The first step was making the decision; the next step was choosing how I was going to use my energy. For me, it meant channeling the energy that used to go into worrying about what I was going to do and how I was going to survive into being as creative a person as I could be. I searched deep inside myself for the meaningful aspects of my life and for ways to do more of what was most meaningful. I discovered this meant doing more teaching, and as I became progressively immersed in this part of my life, I found more and more that I wanted to share with the world. I had a tremendous amount of physical energy available to me to do this because I wasn't trying to depress my energy or using it to sit and worry.

When Anne came to see me, she was suffering from chronic fatigue syndrome, and I did some shamanic healing work with her. She decided that she wanted to learn about shamanism herself and started taking workshops with me. It became clear as I watched her work that she had a particular gift for shamanic work, so I encouraged her to start practicing what she was learning with others. The decision has turned out to benefit all. Not only has she become an incredibly good shamanic practitioner, helping many people, she has also been relieved of her chronic fatigue symptoms. She redirected her energy into helping others, and it worked to heal her.

In my workshops and private work I focus on using the creative energy that is freed up after healing. The good news here is that the healing process makes more energy available. There is bad news, however: That new energy can be used to create bigger illnesses, traumas, and dramas and much faster than in the past.

When I started talking about this concept years ago, I was amazed when many people responded that they had no idea they could create something other than problems in their lives. In our culture we seem to be on a disaster track. How many times have you heard or said, "It's always something." Has it ever occurred to you that it doesn't always have to be "something," that there are different options available to you?

If this thought has not been part of your belief system, you need to back up and examine your life. What would be meaningful to you? People often get stuck on the word *creative* because, for them, it implies making some kind of art, and we all "know" that only a select few are gifted at the creative arts. It is time to evolve out of that belief system. We all have the right to express our soul with pictures, words, actions, dance, or the making of objects, and no person on the planet has the right or the ability to judge the quality and meaningfulness of that creation.

In 1970, when I was in college and rebelling against the world, I remember confronting my English professor. I said, "The paper you gave me a C minus on was something that I wrote from my heart. What gives you the right to judge the words that came from my heart? And is it possible that if some other professor had read that same paper, he or she might have given me an A?" He looked at me as if I were crazy. But he conceded that perhaps another professor might have seen it differently.

I encourage you to use your creative energy to make something that is meaningful to you without the fear of having it judged. Life after healing is about wanting to express your soul in whatever form that takes. One person might decide to take a walk every day instead of sitting around being depressed. Another person might direct energy to the care of plants or creating a garden. You might take a class on a subject that interests you, having no other goal but expanding your knowledge. Maybe you can volunteer your services to help others in a hospital, in a home for the aged, or in a hospice. Perhaps you will devote more of your time to reading, painting, sculpting, writing, or dancing. There are endless ways to use your energy, and you are the only person who knows what would be fun for you at this point in your life. Take a risk, try something. You have nothing to lose in doing this, but you have everything to gain.

Lois described her journey to ask for advice about using her creative energy:

> *I was told that my seven-year journey of healing is about over. I am now to channel my new energies to creative use. I was taken to a beautiful crystal cave, like something in the middle of a geode. A crystal spirit came out to greet me. She told me that I am to make art that has humor, human suffering, and human joy, that it is to be an expression of being in human consciousness. I'm to use handmade netting to represent the web of consciousness like the imagery of the "net of Indra," with a crystal (mirror) at every knot. Every crystal reflects every other crystal. What happens at one is reflected at every other, even to the end of the universe. I'm to make a piece like this about fourteen feet long. It will include imagery that comes from journeying experiences. The crystal spirit will take me on journeys to show me something. I'm to pay attention to what I am shown or experience. I'm to bring that back and put it into an art form that goes into the netting—behind, in front, or woven into it. The netting will be dotted with these experiences from journeys.*
>
> *I'm to trust that it will all work and that it will be exhibited and that it's going to mean something to people.*
>
> *I'm to write about it as it goes along. The narration of the journeys will be part of the piece, for people to understand that this is made from shamanic journeying. This might become a book, in which the closeup photos of the art expression of the journeys and the written account of them are together, an experience that other people can share and understand.*

Welcome Home

Then the crystal spirit wanted to show me something else: Because of human suffering, because it is essential for people to walk through their fear and their pain in order to fully experience the joy of being in human consciousness, I'm to do healing work with them. I am to be the vehicle for the spirit healers who wish to work through me.

All this is the creative use of my energy and the purpose of my own sickness and my own healing. This is the journey I began seven years ago and the outcome of my journey. This is my life from now on. This is my life. I'm to go with it and to trust it and to let it unfold. It will take me into some places that are unexpected, but I'm to know that I will be given the strength to meet the challenges that come. I'm to keep my sense of humor and go with it like a canoe following the current of a river.

Sometimes there will be "white water," and sometimes it will be very serene and tranquil. I'm to trust it and go with it. That is the message. That is the journey. This is my life after healing.

In doing shamanic work with people who are facing life-threatening illnesses, I noticed a significant pattern. People who come to me for a one-time "fix" and refuse to look at making changes in their lives stay well for some time but eventually fall ill again. By contrast, clients who continue their healing process by making the changes that are necessary to make their lives more life-supportive, who decide how to use their creative energy, beat the odds and live good lives. I don't want to simplify the healing process—I see death not as a failure but as one way for us to transform and heal—but my point is this: It is the responsibility of every individual to choose how to create and maintain health in his or her life. And when people are not willing to do this, I'm not sure how their future can change in a positive and significant way.

The keys to creating a healthy present and future are making a conscious decision to do so, trusting that you have the ability to create a good life for yourself, knowing that you deserve the best, and being willing to take action and use your energy in a truly creative way. In my work I teach that the word *power* means the ability to use energy, the ability to transform energy. In life after healing, we are really talking about transforming our energy into creating life-supportive and positive futures, thereby becoming power-filled.

FREEING OURSELVES FROM LIMITING ATTITUDES AND BELIEFS

Often, when we explore being creative, some little annoying voice inside prevents us from moving forward. It's usually a voice from the past that can represent a core belief on which we base our decisions. It might say, "I'm going to get hurt," "I'm not good enough," "There's not enough time," "I don't have enough energy," or "I don't know how"—all those endless phrases that sabotage change.

I like to find out where that core attitude or belief came from. This means going back as far into the past as possible to see the original belief as it became part of our being from our experience at a very early age. Looking at core beliefs is part of the process in all healing, whatever the form of healing. Once that limiting belief has been identified, the next step is to let it go.

A wonderful tool for releasing these beliefs is ritual or ceremony. By itself, ritual creates change. In order to use ritual, one's body, mind, and spirit must get involved. The mind develops the ritual, the body actually performs it, and the spirit acts as a guide and witness at the ritual. This process alerts our psyche that a change is about to occur. So much of our energy goes into preparing and performing the ritual that the psyche takes this act very seriously and follows up by making the appropriate change.

Ritual can be done alone, but one of the ingredients I find helpful is the company of other people. Doing any ritual with a group raises the power of the intention. A group also provides witnesses to what has been done, which heightens the level of commitment for the participants, and it allows community support, a crucial aspect of life after healing. We need to draw like-minded people into our lives who truly support us in our visions and on our path to creating a good life.

I've led a great number of releasing ceremonies for groups and individuals, and I have done my share for myself. I find the use of fire to be a very powerful way of releasing. I would like to share with you how I go about working in this way.

The first step is to find out what the blocking belief, attitude, or issue is at this point in your life. If you know how to do shamanic journeying, journey to a spirit helper who can help you gain access to this information. If you don't journey, just get into a quiet place, go inside yourself, and ask what needs to be released from your life. You might already be aware of the issue through past work that you have done in your healing process.

The next step is to make an object that can be that belief or attitude. You don't want this object to symbolize this belief or attitude; instead, you want this object to *become* this attitude or belief. I've heard Jonathan Horwitz, an anthropologist, say that "shamanic art doesn't symbolize power—shamanic art *is* power."

I suggest you go out into nature. Take a walk and start to collect sticks, grasses, flowers, leaves, and other objects that you can put together into a talisman that will become this limiting belief in your life. Or maybe you want to make something out of things you have in your house. You may want to draw a symbol of what you are releasing on a piece of paper, or else you can just write a description of what you are releasing on the paper. The nature of your object is not what is important; the power and the intention that you put into it is. Please do this step in silence, in a place where you will not be disturbed and where you can concentrate.

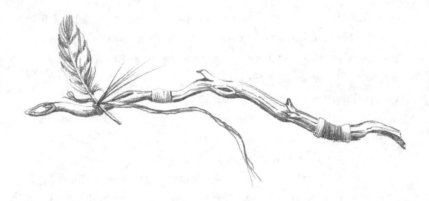

If you decide to do this ceremony with some friends, have everyone go out on their own and take time to make their talismans. At this point do not share what you are releasing. Many of us have the habit of breaking the power of the moment by talking about it. You want the power to build up inside you so you are really ready to let it go.

The next step is to build a fire. Give this some thought, and start to prepare for the fire beforehand. You can use a fire pit in nature if this is available to you. A fireplace is another option. I've even used a small barbecue when there was no other place for me to build a fire. I suggest that you do this at night, because there is a certain power that the darkness adds to doing this work.

If you are doing this ritual alone, bring your power object to be burned with you, and build a fire. If you are part of a group, meet at an appointed time, and build the fire together. This is a sacred ceremony and will mark a day of freedom in your life. You might feel that you want to wear something special, or something that reminds you of your power, or that gives you comfort as you prepare for taking a risk.

At some point, whether it is during the building of the fire or after it is burning, put out a call to the helping spirits of the land to lend support, guidance, and love in the ceremony that is about to begin. Ask them to be witness to your act of freedom on this evening.

Now you are ready to continue with the ceremony. The ceremony actually starts with the original decision and with the making of your object of release. Many healing traditions hold the belief that you must feel in your body what you are releasing before change can occur. The way I do this is by "dancing" the belief or attitude that I am getting ready to let go. It's the last opportunity for me to really feel it and be with it before saying good-bye to it.

If you are performing this ceremony alone, then do this step in your own time. For a group I suggest this be done one at a time. You may feel self-conscious, but in expressing your soul you must allow yourself to be vulnerable.

As you dance, when the feeling is full in your body, let the object that you have been holding go into the fire. Whether it is a piece of paper or some other creation, just let it go. Silently ask for the fire to take this energy and transform it to healing energy. Thank the fire and feed it by putting some cedar or tobacco into the flames, then return to your place in the circle.

The rest of the group could do some drumming, rattling, or humming during this part of the ceremony. The group members might say words of support and congratulations or howl as each person makes this act toward freedom.

These are only suggestions. Ritual loses its power and meaning if it is simply followed like a recipe. It must come from your heart. Make this ritual your own.

I usually use fire when I do releasing ceremonies. Fire has such a transformative quality! I've even burned pieces of paper with words on them in a candle over a sink. There are endless ways to do this work. You could bury the object and, with love and respect, ask the earth to take your belief, or with reverence, ask a body of water like a river, the ocean, or a running stream to take your object.

Know that you cannot make a mistake in coming up with a ritual, and one form will not be more powerful than another. The way you come to the ritual is what creates the power—the intention and commitment, not the form.

Timothy's experience with a fire ceremony illustrates the importance of trust:

> *The fire ceremony was particularly illuminating for me. My three things to cast into the fire were negativity, hopelessness, and despair. I spoke to the fire about how to perform the ritual. What I heard but didn't heed for a while was, "Step into the circle, stare into me, and you will know what to do." I wanted to know what to do before stepping into the circle, but I was unable to come up with anything. Finally I walked into the circle, stared at the fire, and I knew what to do.*
>
> *Basically I was not trusting the fire to speak to me, and I then did not trust its instructions. This was a rich ceremony for me, with lessons in trust and in doing something without always having a plan.*

In *Soul Retrieval* I spoke about how isolated we have become in our lives, and how community really doesn't exist for many of us anymore; I suggested that one find at least one other person to talk to about some of the concepts in the book. In *Welcome Home,* I ask you to take this one step further. Find at least one other person, but preferably two or three other people, who want to move forward in their lives. They are out there. Ask them to come together to create and participate in some ceremony in which all can support one another in continuing their soul's journey.

A ritual done in community has extraordinary power. DCB writes these words:

> *As a single person, I often feel alone but not particularly lonely. During the fire ceremony, the constant drumming and brilliance of the fire transported me into another dimension. By the time I went to dance, there was thick energy inside my body . . . much more energy than I normally possess. I felt drunk, not in control*

of my feet with this vibrant energy pouring through . . . my intention razor sharp, and only partially aware of the community around me. . . . with grass talisman grasped in hand, I plunged it into the fire. . . . there was a cheer from the group and the sound of the drums . . . and I felt exalted by community support . . . for one small moment . . . not alone in the world.

Chaotic joy . . . scream of laughter whirling into me . . . inner wind whipping through, whirling through body, moving into an expression of ecstasy . . . fire and I one . . . . Dissolving with passion that which is no longer needed for the health of consciousness. . . . I knew what it was like to dance like flames in the night. . . . I knew what it was like to be embraced by the goodwill of a community of people.

Annette's experience was quite different:

I have always been terrified of fire— my belief is that it destroys whatever is meaningful. In terms of my life, it has represented passion and energy, both of which I have avoided like death. I've lived out an image of myself as a mountain (the kind that you see in the desert—dry, bald, colorless, the kind you don't want to be close to or explore)—an immovable, passive mound of granite that can withstand whatever comes its way. I think that I was born with joy and liveliness, but I got burned out by other people's passions and desires. Some part of me then erected the facade of stone mountain lady—a survival technique to bury the terrors of night and day. When I prepared for the fire ceremony, I was led to gather the following things: a dirty, rough piece of stone, gathered from the side of the bridge; dead bark; dead leaves; dried pieces of log. These represented the beliefs I had been given in a journey: I would never be free of headaches; to be a woman means to be abused, hurt, destroyed; my body is not good enough to hold health, sex, or spirit—it is a flawed vessel; my "host" or male domineering personality (mountain-symbol) is stronger than my creative, spirited female parts; I'm not capable of speaking or writing clearly. I knew that I had to take off my glasses and leave them on the side of the fire as I stumbled, swinging the rock around the fire. As I felt the heat of the flames, heard the sound of the drums, this voice whispered like the night breeze, "Annette, I will not hurt you. Warmth doesn't need to kill." At that moment I could begin giving up the power struggle I was in, creating excruciating pain, both physically, emotionally, and spiritually to protect against the "invasion," the presence of creation, of spirit. To live means I have to release death and be ignited with passion—burn with life—not out of control but surrounded by stone, trees, people, the circle. My death idol was smashed and replaced with a burning bush.

Christina wrote:

I journeyed for "a belief that blocks me from moving forward in my life that I can release tonight in the fire." My power animal took me to a stream and, gesturing to it, he said, "Your belief is that you are not part of this."

"What is 'this'?" I asked, confused, "a stream?"

"This work, this path, this way, this family . . . ," and he gestured off into infinity. "You have so many animals and so much help, yet you question it. You feel the rightness of your place in this group, yet you question whether it's OK to be in the group. You are part of this."

As I listened I felt clearly that there was no "real" option other than to be part of all that is.

My experience of the Fire Ceremony ritual was quite literal, given the belief "I am not part of this." I filled my body and consciousness with the belief that I was not part of the group. I felt myself withdraw, and I could hardly drum in rhythm with everyone as we started. I realized that this growing feeling of isolation and loneliness was familiar. I was surprised by the pain; I was not aware of how painful these familiar feelings were until

I stood there, in that moment. This whole experience of not belonging heightened quickly as it became harder and harder to drum with the group. I had to step into the circle and didn't even make it all the way around the fire; my body became immobilized by the paralysis that this belief brings to my life. I threw my talisman into the fire, and it tangled in my hair, making my desire to be rid of it even more intense. My experience of the final release into the fire is hard to find words for. My healing began, quite literally, after I stepped back into the circle and began drumming again.

As completely as I was filled with pain and isolation before, I was filled now with the drumming and the unity of "group" created through the beat. I was first aware of being part of the beat. Next I was aware of supporting the members of the group in their release. Then slowly I was aware of being part of the group. When I got that, my mind slipped through all the times in my life that I had been part of a spiritual group around the fire: our Unitarian Church campouts, family camps, moon ceremonies—all of which I had forgotten. And when the drumming was silent, I was still part of the group. I heard the stream flowing behind me, and I heard my power animal saying, "You are part of this," and I knew from the experience in my bones that this was true.

I was also moved by Matthew's experience:

The Fire Ceremony was very powerful for me and a fitting climax to the week.

On the journey beforehand to find out what attitude or belief was preventing me from using my creative energy, my teacher had told me that it was the belief that I was not my own person that I had to let go of. This black hole of neediness within me she gave to me to burn in the fire in the form of a black ring. So after the journey I looked in the forest for something in the shape of a black ring. I ran up the hill to my favorite two birch trees and asked them where to look. They said, "At our feet," and there indeed—despite my inescapable skepticism at the validity of talking with trees—was the perfect talisman: A black piece had fallen from the one with the rotted trunk. Those trees are my brothers.

During the ceremony I was only intermittently conscious of what everyone else was doing. My black talisman had begun to hold the memory of my worst feeling—when I had lain on my bed at night in my tidy apartment in New York, feeling like a turtle must feel with a skewer run under his shell and right up through his heart. Tears came down my cheeks; my legs and my whole body were weak. I stepped into the circle and fell in the dirt and lay in a fetal position in the dark beneath my coat, remembering how I thought I would never be able to sleep again. Then I got up, placed the talisman in the fire, and started to dance around the fire facing outward toward everybody— because, having let go of my pain, I wanted the power to dance with other people. At first I shook my rattle at them with little result, but by the time I had gone completely around the circle I had learned how to entice people to rattle, dance, and hoot with me. I was so happy I could have danced all night—but I stepped out of the circle for the next person to enter. After that I could watch other people let go of their pain as everybody drummed and whooped louder and louder. I wish we could have gone on till dawn. The bright joy of it still burns in my breast.

In freeing ourselves from words, beliefs, and attitudes that block us, we choose the path of life. We free ourselves to create from a clean slate, from a belief that all things are possible. This act takes a tremendous amount of courage, just as creating a future free from our past wounds takes a tremendous amount of courage. It means being a pioneer and a visionary. It can be exciting to think about all the opportunities you can create for yourself.

Basically, I ask you to stretch beyond what you think you are capable of doing, to release any negative parenting or role models in your life that instilled in you any limiting beliefs or ideas. As a species, we have not yet begun to tap into our creative potential. Give yourself more credit now than you have in the past, and know you are capable of so much more. Be open to the exciting possibilities to create harmony and joy in your life.

In *Soul Retrieval* I wrote that the key to understanding shamanism is intention and trust: being clear on what you are asking for and knowing that the spirits will be there to answer your call. In *Welcome Home,* I am not only asking you to trust the spirits, but more important, I am asking you to trust yourself. Trust your own spirit. Know that if you form a clear intention about what and how you want to create, your own spirit will support you and bring you to your goals.

MORE ABOUT COMMUNITY SUPPORT

In *Soul Retrieval* I wrote about how important community was in shamanic societies to support the healing process for all individuals. Now I would like to take the concept of community one step further.

After my healing process from depression I felt wide awake all the time. When I was absorbed in my own problems, I was only vaguely aware of the world around me. My energy was directed to my internal problems, and I could not give my full attention to what was going on around me.

After healing, when my energy was free to engage fully in the world, I could no longer "numb out" to what was happening outside myself. Whether I was looking at the bigger picture of the world at large, or at my community, or at my close relationships, I found myself wide awake. What I discovered is that not everyone in my life and in the world had chosen to heal.

In some ways I felt more isolated than I remembered ever feeling, as though I was looking at a world that was unconscious and asleep, going through the motions of life. Here I was, after so many years of being depressed, with all this newfound energy to create life in a different way. I wanted to have people around me with like minds. I needed to have people around me to mirror the state of growth I had moved to instead of reflecting my own past wounds of separation, abandonment, betrayal, and fear. I saw the world with new eyes, and I wanted to be with other people who also saw the incredible beauty I was experiencing. I realized how much the earth and being alive had to offer, and I wanted to share that excitement and play with others in this earth garden.

Community took on a different meaning for me. I no longer sought community I could commiserate with. Instead, I wanted community I could be awake with and talk with about building a better place to live. I wanted people around me who could be a "reality check." I find it a challenge to stay centered in a world that seems to put most of its creative energy into destruction. In my life I wanted people whose presence reminded me of my strength and the unlimited creative potential that I have, a community that could encourage and inspire.

Having an intention to create a healthy community around me and trusting that I had the ability to create what I needed in my life brought many rewards for my labor. I found an abundance of people who were in a similar place, not people one would consider "perfect" or "enlightened" beings. Often we look for unrealistic role models in our lives. We look for perfection instead of acceptance of who we are. The people I found myself attracting into my life were people who also wanted to redirect their energy. I found people who were tired of creating drama.

I know there are people who are looking at a new way of thinking, looking toward a brighter future, or I wouldn't be writing this book. So I encourage you to look around at the community you have created. Are you with people who support your growth process? If you are, that is great. If you find yourself feeling a need to make a change, do it. Start with putting out a strong intention to find people to mirror back the healing work that you have done. Next, trust that your own spirit will start to attract those people into your life. If you still don't trust yourself, do a ritual or ceremony like the ones I suggest in this chapter to let go of your limiting beliefs. I have total faith in you and your creative potential. Trust yourself. We all need people in our lives who can be a support system for us as we start to create positive futures in a world that collectively has not yet come to a place of healing. It takes a lot of strength to stay centered in the chaos of the world today as the natural process demands that we grow, change, and transform.

A few years ago, when the United States decided to go to war with Iraq, I journeyed to Isis. I asked her what I should be doing during this time. I knew that I couldn't change things, but I wanted to know how I should behave or how to improve my attitude. The message she gave me was quite profound: "Some people have to be willing to tend the garden while all the destruction is going on." That message really stuck with me, and it echoes in my ears daily as I travel around the country teaching and as I watch the world around me. I have made a choice to be a "garden tender," no matter what is going on around me. And as others still feel a need to destroy, I have found it crucial to support those who continue to garden and tend to life.

It takes a lot of energy to create an illness, a trauma, or a drama. You have the choice to redirect your creative energy to manifesting life-supportive situations and relationships.

Power is the ability to use and transform energy.

We can use ritual or ceremony as a way to release any limiting beliefs or attitudes we are holding onto that block us from using our creative potential.

It is important to have a community that supports us as we evolve to a more positive place—a community that will mirror back who we really are and our visions, even while the rest of the world is creating destruction.

We must continue to tend the garden no matter what is going on around us.

Thoughts to ponder:

> *When we free ourselves from our limiting beliefs, we free our ancestors who passed these on to us. In this way, healing takes place in the past, the present, and the future.*
>
> *You can't kill energy. You have to transform it.*

EXERCISES

1. How do you want to use your creative energy?

2. What are the attitudes or negative beliefs blocking you from using your creative potential?

3. Create a ritual for releasing these attitudes or beliefs. Invite two or more friends, co-workers, family members, or anyone else whom you would like to share this work with and do this ritual together.

4. What kind of people would you like to call your community? Write down and make clear to yourself some of the qualities you are looking for in a community.

5. Create a community of power objects around you. Make a special place in your house where you can keep objects you have found or that were given to you as gifts that can remind you of your power and help you keep centered when you need a reminder of who you are.

Within the gentle gift
of youthful joy
and being
once known
then lost.
I found myself
and knew again
my mind
my thoughts
washed clean
Made new
Although
remembered faintly
through the fog of time.

I hugged the self
I had not known
so long
but welcomed back
into my arms
so sweetly.

Feelings long gone
sprang anew
from my breast
like
secret flowers
hidden
in dark places
so happy
to see
sunlight
again.

—Harriet Toben

CHAPTER 6

KNOW YOURSELF

The 1990s are a time of great change and transformation, and change often plunges people into a state of fear. Because of fear of the unknown, many people want to control their own lives—as well as the lives of others. We are conditioned in many ways to believe that change is bad; however, we are a part of nature, unable to separate ourselves from the natural world, and nature is in constant change. Change means evolution and growth.

Control is not the solution to the changes needed in our decade. The ability to flow and stay centered is the key to positive change. The key to staying centered in the midst of fear and chaos is to know yourself: to know your boundaries, beliefs about right and wrong, and personal ethics. To stay in a place of integrity and speak your truth is what is needed, and to be compassionate with yourself and with the world around you.

To do all this, you must be in right relationship with yourself. This means that you must be able to say no to those who try to control and block the process of evolution and transformation by choosing fear over change. The beginning of the transformation that must occur involves saying yes to what is life-supportive for you. Only you know what changes are right for you and your life. To create a positive future you must take back your power and state what is so from a place of self-knowledge. Ask for your lessons and your growth to come from a place of gentleness and kindness. Know that what is coming is not too big to handle.

Although in this culture we have been trained to give away our power, it is our responsibility—on both an individual and a collective level—to make things better for us. I see many people around me looking to the government, to religious leaders, to science to create a better reality. How can an outside force create a better reality, when it is we as adults who create that reality? In the "New Age" I watch in amazement as people wait for the mothership from another planet or galaxy to come down and magically heal the earth and its inhabitants.

As adults we must take responsibility for what we have created, and if we don't like what is happening, we must change it. I do not believe that we should wait for "something bigger and wiser" than we are to clean up our mess and create miracles for us. For me, the "second coming" means finding the "Christ consciousness" of love and compassion and the knowledge of how to heal ourselves. We must learn to know ourselves, grow up, express our souls, and take back the power to change illness, pollution, and destruction into a world full of meaning, passion, and compassion for all.

Self-knowledge is the first step—knowing who you are. This means being honest instead of judging yourself. One of the concepts running rampant in the New Age is that of unconditional love. I do believe that in time the human race can evolve to a place of unconditional love. But where are we right now? As a species, we have strong egos. Those strong egos are needed to keep us alive today, to survive the abuse and dysfunction surrounding us. Unfortunately, it is our egos that have created that same abuse and dysfunction. But we have to get to know our egos, accept their voices, learn to use them in balance with Spirit, and not let ego rule the world. Though unconditional love perhaps cannot be part of our reality at this time, compassion for ourselves can be. But we cannot continue to deny our behavior. We must look at our behavior with as much honesty as we can muster and then look at how we can change any destructive behavior we embrace. A person with a knowledge of self is capable of evolving to a higher place. People who deny who they are create an illusion of who they are and therefore cannot move forward.

Some of what I say in this chapter might be controversial. I am taking a risk in sharing some of my opinions, which might be misunderstood. My intention, however, is to challenge you. I want to challenge you to stretch yourself on the emotional, physical, and spiritual levels. Everything I say to you I say to myself, and as a self-knowing adult, you have the right to accept or reject anything I say.

In doing shamanic work with people in workshops and with individual clients, I see two pitfalls. One is with people who have been doing a lot of "inner child" work, either through shamanic soul retrieval, hypnosis, or other psychological methods. People get stuck in the process of integration. In *Soul Retrieval* I ask readers to journey to their retrieved parts, meet them, and get to know their needs. Although this journey might not be a one-time experience, I don't believe it should be a lifetime experience. A woman once introduced herself to me like this: "My adult part is delighted to meet you; my thirteen-year-old is terrified to meet you; and please excuse my five-year-old. She is painfully shy."

The point of healing work is integration, not more fragmentation. Yes, it is important to meet aspects of yourself and get to know them, but they are you—an adult who has the tools to take care of the frightened and shy parts. A creative person is one unit—made up of body, mind, and spirit—having one goal in life: to create the healthiest life possible.

I am certain you know yourself. Ask yourself honestly if you still need time to work on your integration process. Or is it time for you to accept that your parts are "home" and it's now time for you to become integrated as one creative being? No one except you can make this decision. No one can judge you for where you are in your process. Make that process conscious, and decide where you are and what you need.

The second pitfall of doing any spiritual work is confusion about what is information that comes from ego and what is spiritual guidance. It's crucial to understand this difference when we talk about setting boundaries and life after healing. When your own boundaries are unclear, you may be confused about what is spiritual guidance and what is coming from the ego. I feel strongly that to successfully move forward on a spiritual path, we must put aside what the ego wants and go to a deeper place where Spirit can speak.

I sometimes see people hiding behind Spirit to express their needs. There is a qualitative difference between information that our helping spirits bring and information that the ego brings. If you are on a spiritual path, you need to know the difference. In a group, when a person says, "Spirit said . . . ," and this information cuts off other people's sharing of experiences, I question where that information came from. When someone announces that "Spirit's decision is . . . ," I question where that decision came from as well.

All that I know of spiritual traditions is that Spirit doesn't have "control issues." Spirit doesn't give orders, and Spirit is not codependent. Spirit shows us our choices and what is involved in making those choices; Spirit accommodates everyone's experience.

In knowing yourself, it is important to know your needs and desires. It is not an act of integrity to hide behind a spiritual being to express yourself. You must have the courage and the willingness to express what you need, and you must understand that what you need cannot always be accommodated by whomever you are with at the time. It takes a lot of courage and strength to be willing to be that honest with yourself.

Years ago when I had a full-time shamanic counseling practice, I decided to try an experiment to help myself become the best shamanic practitioner that I could be. After listening to a person's issue, I would then do the journey appropriate for him or her at that time. I shared my experiences with my clients afterward in two ways. I would say, "These are my personal thoughts on your issue, and this is the spiritual guidance I received for you." I carefully watched my results. I found a qualitative difference in the information that was coming directly from me versus the information that I was receiving in nonordinary reality. With practice I became able to know who was talking. Over and over, I found that the information I obtained in nonordinary reality was more helpful and profound than the information that came from my own thought process. I learned how to tell the difference between ego and spiritual guidance. Although it was often humbling, it was important for me to have this experience, and I certainly gained an understanding of myself and of the difference between spiritual guidance and what was coming from my ego. I am no longer in danger of intruding into my own spiritual practice, because I have learned the difference between the two.

I also learned the appropriate questions to ask for spiritual guidance and how to phrase my questions to get the richest, deepest answers. As an adult, I am responsible for certain decisions in my life. For example, a question such as "Should I be in a relationship with so-and-so?" does not work in my own life. Asking questions of "should I?" gives away my own creative power. The question I have found to give me great insight and help is, "What lessons are there for me about being in a relationship with so-and-so?" By phrasing my question this way, I get so much information about the positive aspects of my possible choice as well as the negative consequences that the "should" part becomes irrelevant. Another good question is, "Would this choice be life-supportive, or would I be creating a new drama in my life?" In this way I work in partnership with the spirits, and I don't give my power away to some outside force.

In life after healing, it's important to distinguish between the information that comes from within yourself and information that comes from outside. And it's just as important to know when that information will allow choices that are for the highest good of all concerned or whether those choices will be creating another drama in your life. These are big issues. The answer is to use discipline in your spiritual work, to practice, and to watch your results with brutal honesty. Know your own emotional needs and desires so they don't invade your work in dysfunctional ways. Take care of your body so it is strong enough to house your spirit as you grow and evolve in a spiritual way. Start bringing into ordinary reality the dreams and visions that are coming through.

Know yourself well enough to be honest with yourself and those around you. This concept becomes even more crucial when we talk about bringing the soul back into business, but it is also important in manifesting our creativity, for we want to fully align what we are asking for on an unconscious level with what we request on a conscious level. Otherwise, when we become better at using our creative energy, we might re-create what our unconscious minds have kept in denial.

We must reach a place of being able to state our needs and to discern what is appropriate at a particular time for us as whole, responsible adults.

HOW DO YOU RECEIVE INFORMATION?

A key to working successfully with spiritual practice is learning and understanding how you personally receive information.

In one of the exercises at the end of chapter 2, you noted how you receive with your ordinary senses. There are also nonordinary senses with which we receive. The senses that are strongest in both ordinary and nonordinary reality vary from person to person.

Over the past ten years, as I have taught people how to journey, I have been fascinated to note that the sense they use to receive information in ordinary reality is not necessarily their strongest sense in nonordinary reality. For example, in ordinary reality I cannot learn through listening. If I am trying to learn a foreign language, I must see the words; I cannot learn even a single word through listening. Likewise, when I listen to a lecture, I find that at the end of the lecture I can't recall one word. But in nonordinary reality and in my dreams, my *best* sense is listening. The most powerful messages and lessons I have received have been through words, and visual information has almost no meaning for me. I get information visually when I am journeying for another person because most people relate best to visual images. When I am journeying for myself, however, I almost never see strong visions.

One of the most frustrating populations for me to teach shamanic journeying to is artists. In ordinary reality, artists tend to be very visual, but I often find that they do not see visually in their shamanic journeys. If I can get them to validate the other senses they are "seeing" with, they have extraordinary experiences. I know many artists who experience their journeys through feeling the information, yet back in ordinary reality describe what they felt with visual words.

As a culture we are so stuck in the visual aspect of both ordinary and nonordinary reality that we tend to invalidate information that comes through other senses. This makes me feel sad, for I don't believe that the visual is our most evolved sense. I believe that the earth communicates directly with us and that the visual information we receive is only intermediary.

One of my challenges in teaching shamanism is to get people to validate their own mode of receiving information and not to compare their mode of "seeing" to other people's. I encourage them in whatever form of spiritual practice they have—it might not be shamanism—to open all their senses to how they personally are experiencing the information. Part of knowing oneself is discovering how information is received in ordinary and nonordinary ways.

Besides knowing what senses are the strongest in ordinary reality and nonordinary reality, there are other aspects to consider. How do you personally learn best? Are you a person who needs to find a teacher in ordinary reality to work with, or do you learn best from your own spirit helpers? In my own life I find I always learn best through my shamanic journeys, dreams, and intuitions. I know other people who learn best through reading and taking classes. Again, the way you learn is very personal. One way is not better than another—the important question is, What is best for you?

Do you learn best by meditating, shamanic journeying, or through dreams? Are you a person who needs to sit still when you are engaged in a spiritual practice, or do you learn more through movement? Do you learn best by being silent, or by sharing your thoughts with others? When I can speak about what I am working on or write down my thoughts, my perceptions are amazing. Yet I know many people who need to retreat to a place of silence to deepen the insights they are receiving.

These ideas about learning are very important, because they relate to developing a strong relationship with self. As you get to know yourself better and consider these questions, you will find that your own creativity expands significantly. You will have more confidence in yourself and in your own abilities as you discover where your strengths are.

Above all, please stay flexible when exploring your learning and receiving modes. We all change. As you continue your own spiritual practice and pursue creativity, you might find that different ways work for you at different times and that sometimes all ways will work for you.

For me, the more I learn about myself, my ego needs, and my spiritual and creative strengths, the easier it is to maintain my boundaries and stay centered when I find myself surrounded by chaos or destructive situations. Because we live in a time of such change, expansion, and transformation, it is easy to understand that our reactions will vary from day to day and in different groups of people. Remember who you are and stay centered so that you will always know what appropriate action or behavior is needed. In this time of great change:

- Stay focused

- Stay positive

- Stay centered.

DEALING WITH PROBLEMS AS THEY ARISE

Life after healing does not mean a life in which you will never again have any issues to work on; healing is a lifelong process. But at some point energy must be directed away from our healing process so we can move on with our lives. There will always be opportunities to work on issues even as we shift our attention to our creative process.

Recently, at a workshop, a wonderful man who has been studying with me for a while came up to me during a break wondering if he could ask me a personal question. When I said, "Of course," he asked me how I heal myself. He has taken many healing workshops with me and knows my feelings about the importance of getting outside help for illness, but I gathered his question had a different meaning.

From the perspective of life after healing, this is what I do to heal myself: When I have an emotional or physical problem that I don't feel needs outside intervention, there are a couple of ways I work in behalf of myself. The most common way is to ask for a healing dream every night before I go to bed. I have never done any formal work with dreams, but on my own I have discovered that a lot can be learned from them. I often get help for myself in dreams, and all my life I have been told by others that they were healed by me in a dream.

About ten years ago, I had a very painful physical condition. At the time, I lived in San Francisco, where I had an abundance of medical specialists to turn to. They reported that my case was untreatable and that I would have to get used to living with the pain. I had people journey for me shamanically. It didn't help. I had psychic readings; they didn't help either. I tried every outside source of traditional and alternative healing that I could find. The prospect of living with the pain did not feel like a viable option for me.

Every night before I went to sleep, I prayed for help in a dream. This was an act of desperation; nothing else that I knew of was helping. I asked diligently every night for months. One night I had the most extraordinary dream: I dreamed that I was in the living room of my house. Suddenly a young, handsome Native American man appeared from behind my couch dressed in blue jeans and a blue work shirt. In his hand was a rattle made of an extraordinary skin that was a translucent blue, just like the blue color of my protective egg. He said that he always lived here and that I just didn't know it. He pointed his finger at the place in my body where I was experiencing all my pain and said, "You have a problem right here." He shook his rattle over the diseased part of my body. At that moment I could actually feel the pain lift out of my body. I knew inside the dream that I had had a healing and that I would be free of the pain forever. The man disappeared at that point. Indeed, I did awaken from the dream pain-free and have been free of this problem ever since. One could say that this was actually me doing the healing or that there was actually an outside spirit who came to my aid. I do not give any thought to that. I just know that the dream worked, and I am always thankful to whoever appeared to help me.

From that day forth, I have turned to my dreams for help. A healing dream doesn't always come on the first try, but if I keep asking, it comes eventually. I use my dreams for both emotional and physical issues. If I am very disturbed by something emotionally, I ask for help with it in my dreams. At first I might get very chaotic dreams about this issue, as my psyche or the spirits present different aspects of the issue to me, but then the dreams become clearer. I use no dream interpretation, because I find it just absorbs me into my past again. Instead, I take my dreams literally and ask for information that will be healing for me. In this way, I stay forward-looking as I work.

The other way that I work in my own behalf is to put out a telepathic call to my helping spirits for assistance with a specific situation. I won't always do a formal journey; sometimes I just call out and ask for help. I have found that I get extraordinary results with this.

I use both these methods for myself as well as in working with people long-distance. Sometimes, instead of using one of the traditional shamanic healing methods, I will ask for a healing dream to be sent to the person who asked me for help, or else I will silently ask for my helping spirits to send help. I do this only after the person on whose behalf I am working has asked me. I never take another's healing process into my own hands unless that person asks me to intervene. Doing healing work without a person's permission is the greatest psychic intrusion I can imagine. I know that I don't want anyone invading my psychic space for any reason without my permission, whether it's to harm me or to help me. This is an issue of boundaries and knowing who you are. When you know who you are, you can tell when to ask for outside help and when to go within yourself and do your own healing. Life after healing means taking an adult stance and asking for what you need.

SOUL REMEMBERING

One day as I was doing a soul retrieval with a client, as I was nearly done with my journey and ready to come back with the soul parts that I had gathered with my power animal, my power animal suddenly said that there was one more part that I had to bring back. He took me back to a part that held the gift and strength of my client. My power animal instructed me to bring that part back. I felt I needed to question him at that point.

"Paul didn't lose this part through any trauma, did he?"

"No," my power animal responded.

"Well, if he didn't lose this part to trauma, how am I supposed to bring it back? How do I bring back something that was never lost?"

My power animal had a particular look on his face that he gets when he is about to teach me something new. He said, "Paul did not lose this part through a trauma, but he has forgotten this part. And this part is essential for his own healing process at this time. So what I want you to do is to go back before this part ever came in. I want you to go back as Paul was coming into the world with this gift and talent and take it back to him along with the lost soul parts we retrieved."

I went back as far as I could into Paul's birthing process and looked for this part. It contained not only the beauty and presence with which Paul came into this world, but also the unlimited light that he needed to help with the physical illness he was dealing with right now. I found a huge globe of gold light. I asked my power animal if this was what I was to take. He answered, "Yes." At that point I left nonordinary reality, following my power animal's instructions, and blew all the parts back into Paul.

What my power animal explained to me during a later journey was that what he was teaching me was not soul retrieval; it had to do with blowing in a soul part that had been forgotten and was needed back for a person's emotional or physical healing. Because it's a part that has not been lost, just forgotten, I call this process "soul remembering."

I don't do this process on all clients as a standard part of a soul retrieval. Instead I wait until my power animal instructs me to do so. He has asked me to do this with about 10 percent of my clients. Two separate times when I performed a soul remembering as part of the soul retrieval, I brought back the forgotten essence as a five-pointed star. Both the women for whom I returned them said their houses were decorated with five-pointed stars.

Among the clients I spoke with, the soul part remembered as a symbol had great significance to them. It served as a reminder of both who they were and the strength that they could tap into at any time. Along with the symbol, my power animal also gives me the words to accompany that strength or gift. For example, I might learn that a person's strength is his or her solidity and centeredness and the symbol is a tree. Or I will be told that a person's strengths or gifts in this lifetime are the ability to love and a sense of compassion; for this, the symbol might be a heart. One of the things I like about being given the symbol as well as the words is that the picture can easily be empowering and remembered by bringing it into conscious awareness or by drawing a picture of it that one can look at regularly as a reminder.

In one workshop where I taught this process, an interesting synchronicity occurred. In the assignment the shamanic practitioner was to pick someone in the workshop to do the soul remembering with and then after the journey come back and draw in color the symbol for that person. At the end of the exercise one of the participants shared that there were two other workshop participants with whom she had found herself spending a significant amount of time during the week. She felt a real camaraderie with these people and felt that they had energies similar to hers. When all three of these people showed me the pictures that were drawn for them as their soul essences, they were almost identical. During the workshop, their own soul essences were being mirrored back to each of them in the presence of the others and caused a natural attraction of like souls.

I would like to share some of the feedback I have gotten from this experience. Another workshop leader, Christina, wrote:

> Susan retrieved my soul's essence, which has allowed me a deeper and clearer connection with my soul's purpose. This connection shows in my eyes in some way that others can see. I know this only because many have commented on it directly since the close of the retreat. My companion, who was angry with me when I returned, said that even through his anger, he experienced a kind of softness in me that he has seen before only in people with a deep sense of purpose and connection to Oneness. He feels that this softness allowed him to move through the anger that he had been holding for weeks. With my essence returned, I led, alone, a retreat of my own design that followed no one else's teaching, and it was "successful" beyond my wildest dreams.

DCB writes:

> In the last ceremony, where we were to find a symbol for the soul before it had experienced trauma in this life, we were journeying for a man who does healing work. The power animals led me to the Upper World. There we found a huge violet-colored eye, with flowers blooming instantly around it and animals

coming toward it—a little bunny, to be exact. Upon return, I
was a little embarrassed to report this Disney-like scene and told
him [the client] that perhaps his gift for others in life was to
allow them to bloom in his presence. I told him about the eye,
and he asked me about its color. When I described the violet
color, he remarked that he had seen this eye many times in his
own meditation, and when it appeared he knew this was his
truth and the path to follow.

This gentleman saw me as a seven-pointed star with whirling
pink and orange energy and with the yin and yang balanced on
the top and bottom. I continually draw a whirling energy and
happened to have a drawing of it that matched somewhat, and
my life has been to seek balance—not exactly successfully, but it
does keep one adventuring into new realms.

Pirrko's soul-remembering journey for her partner involved
a vivid visual experience:

My power animal and I journeyed to a vast space where we saw
my partner's soul essence—a beautiful, living, luminous flower,
mostly lilac in color and shaped something like both a lotus and
an orchid. The petals were not thin, but "fleshy" and each petal
had a life of its own. It was slowly "sailing" through space, like
a magnificent tropical fish. One could see through the petals—
they were vibrating with various hues of lilac, pink, violet. This
flower was emanating a light of its own. In scooping up the
flower in both of my hands, I felt that it was a living being, and
I had to be very careful in handling it.

This is the point of soul remembering for me—adventuring
into new realms of remembering who we are, what gifts we came
here with, and what our soul's purpose is and seeing that our
journey thus far is just a path that brings us to where we are now
and the opportunity that presents in our lives.

THE WOUNDED HEALER

Wounded healer is a shamanic term often used to describe a person who is called to the healing path. In traditional shamanic societies, the wounded healer experienced a near-death episode, a psychotic break, or a life-threatening illness. When someone has had an experience like this and returns to a normal life again, that person can understand the territories to be traveled in healing others.

I believe that all of us who have made it to adulthood are in some sense wounded healers. We have experienced a variety of emotional and physical problems that allow us to have empathy for others who are suffering. Suffering brings us to compassion. I don't know how one can be successful at healing—whether it be with individuals, groups, or friends and family—if compassion is absent. The only way to heal is by having compassion for oneself and others.

In life after healing, it is important to remember where we started. Those of us who have the courage to move forward will be able to help others as long as we can be truly compassionate in our daily interactions with people. Although on the surface the ego can interfere in this process, we must embrace compassion deep in our being. There will be days when we are challenged by those who themselves have forgotten how to be compassionate. Compassion is the key to healing ourselves and the planet and creating a positive future.

Change is part of nature. We live in a time of great change and transformation.

To know our boundaries, our beliefs, and our ethics is very important.

As individuals we have the ability to change our destructive path to a path that supports life. No one outside ourselves can do this for us. We are responsible for creating a positive future for ourselves.

It is important to have strong boundaries when you pursue a spiritual path. Strong boundaries keep you from confusing information that is coming from your own ego with spiritual guidance.

In order to move forward with our lives, and tap into our creative potential, we must see ourselves as one whole unit, not a person made up of fragmented, hurt parts. We must integrate into one functioning adult with different options and strengths than we had in the past.

To know ourselves, we must acknowledge and validate how we learn best: what senses we receive information from and whether we learn better from teachers in ordinary reality or from our own spirit helpers, through silence or through sharing, through being still or through movement.

We must remain flexible with regard to ourselves and our healing process so that we give ourselves permission to keep changing and evolving.

Part of being on a spiritual path is knowing what kind of spiritual guidance to ask for and knowing when we need to take responsibility and be in our own power.

Dreams can be a way of receiving healing as well as a call to one's spirit helpers for aid.

We each came into this world with inherent gifts and strengths. It is time to remember and acknowledge who we truly are.

Having suffered emotionally and/or physically leads to the path of the wounded healer and the gift of compassion.

Thoughts to ponder:

> *Angie Arrien, a shamanic teacher, says that according to the Basque people, "We are all walking stars on a great big giant star."*

> *Compassion is a key to healing and creating a positive future for all life.*

EXERCISES

1. Because getting to know yourself is a crucial part of setting boundaries and being creative, it might be time for you to deepen your own self-knowledge. One way to do this is to see yourself as a plant. In order for your growing process to continue, you must determine what your needs are. What are your desires? You can make a list, write a poem, sing a song, create an object that represents your needs and desires, or do a drawing.

2. Try to think about the qualitative difference you experience when your ego is talking and when Spirit is talking. Write down some of the qualities of each.

3. In this chapter I write about different ways of learning. How do you learn best?

> What senses do you use the most in ordinary reality to receive information?

> What are the invisible senses you use to receive spiritual information?

> Do you learn best from others?

> Do you learn best through your own experience?

> Do you learn best by being still or by being active?

Do you learn best by being silent or by sharing with others?

4. If you are trying to deal with an emotional or physical issue in your life right now, try asking for a healing dream before you go to sleep, or try simply putting out a call to the spirit world to help with what you are working on.

5. Think about yourself and your strengths and gifts. Draw a symbol or a picture that you can put up somewhere in your house to serve as a visual affirmation of who you really are.

CHAPTER 7

BRINGING BACK THE SOUL OF BUSINESS, OUR COMMUNITIES, AND THE EARTH

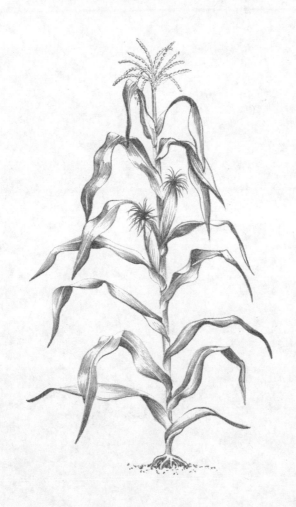

Once you have made significant progress in your healing process, it is time to turn your attention out to the world at large. Marah, a doctor who studied with me, said "It's hard to write about 'after healing' as the healing process never ends. Both as a doctor and as a 'patient' I seem to notice more of a transition from self-focus to other-than-self focus, or world-focus, as more and more of the fracturedness melds and heals. It's a balance; just as I feel I have healed the last big wound, I find a new level of healing and awareness and consequently 'new work' to be done."

As we heal and wake up to the world around us, we need to work on making changes in our earth community that will support life. What we learn through shamanism and other spiritual systems is that all life is sacred and needs respect.

When we look at our business community we find a different message is being broadcast. Money is more important than life. People are overworked and put into hazardous working conditions—all in order to keep profits high. All life forms on the planet as well as the earth itself suffer because money goes before ethics. What is right doesn't matter. Business is concerned about costs and profits.

What business doesn't understand is that the cost of operating in this way has been higher than imaginable. There will be a high price to pay in the future for each individual involved in a business without spirit or soul. It will be painful to have to admit that, indeed, one was part of that culture which exterminated sacred trees or wiped out a whole species of animal for the sake of money, money that never brought real happiness or meaning to life.

I heard a vice president of a major corporation say, "The goal of business is to have a profit." Why isn't the goal of business to provide a service? The emphasis must be taken off money and put back into creativity and life's needs. Money is an exchange of energy. If a business is truly providing a service, then there will be an exchange for that. Money should not be the end goal. Look what a mess we have created on the planet because of it.

Some businesses convince people they need their services by instilling fear in their consumers or clients. If a business truly has a beneficial service to offer, I see no need for using scare tactics to get customers.

When we consider life after healing, we emphasize "win-win" situations because we know that we do have the power to create them.

If we look at what is happening astrologically in 1993 and 1994, we see Uranus and Neptune going conjunct. The last time these planets were conjunct was 170 years ago. Astrologers differ in interpreting how this will affect our planet in the 1990s. Change is inevitable. A couple of years ago I listened to a taped lecture of astrologer Robert Myers, who said that the last time Uranus and Neptune went conjunct marked the beginning of the Industrial Revolution. He said that for the last 170 years we have had business without soul. Now we are looking for the next 170 years to bring the soul back into business. He said this will not be an overnight process. I agree that this change will not be quick. However, I think that because time seems so speeded up for all of us, we can make the transition faster.

I am sure of this: We must begin to change our business behavior. We can no longer afford to value money over life. We must start thinking of our own generation as well as future generations.

We know the problem. What are some positive thoughts that we can bring to creating positive change? In my heart I know that if we provide a service, we will be rewarded for that service. Our end goal should be service, not money. This is nature. This shift to being service-oriented not money-oriented takes a huge leap of faith and trust. It means trusting nature in the largest sense of the word and trusting the natural cycle of life and getting away from the artificial laws that humans have invented. These laws keep us from following our own soul's journey. On a daily basis we are being asked to sell our souls for money.

This issue is big, and the changes will not come overnight. How do we keep our sanity during this time of transition? What are some steps that will move us closer to our goals of inspiring business with integrity and compassion?

One important principle is the concept of partnership and the necessity of expanding the number of people we include in that partnership. Partnership involves all the people who work to develop a particular service. There are small, entrepreneurial companies such as Southwest Airlines, Ben & Jerry's, and Tom's of Maine that already embrace this concept and treat all the workers as partners. They are financially successful, and they are operating with compassion and integrity.

When I work with a client who is getting ready to have surgery, I give that person a piece of advice. "When you go into the hospital, see that the doctors don't have power over you and your body. Consider them partners who are working with you to create a healthy body. See your doctor as your partner in doing this."

In life after healing we cannot take the stance of victim or buy into the belief of "power-over." We must begin to see that we are all partners in creating a good life with one another on this planet. We need to stand together as a community and state what does and does not support life for all our children.

One way to bring the soul back into business is to devote more of our creative energy to the development of business and to the service being provided, exploring how all aspects of that service are oriented to preserving and helping life. We need to create meaningful work for all people who engage in providing service. We can also go to the next step and bring spiritual work into business.

How many people in the business world have worked enough on understanding their ego and will? Would the practice of bringing Spirit into businesses be abused? Would we hear someone say, "Spirit said to raise the price on our product"?

Spiritual guidance should not be used to increase wealth. Instead it should be the basis for ethics and for understanding cycles and the effects of decisions on the rest of the community. This guidance should be used to discover what is necessary for the highest good of all concerned—not for power-over or for greed.

When bringing spirituality into business it is more important than ever to know the difference between ego and Spirit. The best way to distinguish between the two is to concentrate on the service aspect of work as a spiritual and natural path to take. Directing energy and focus onto a monetary goal means falling back into materialism. Have you done this? If so, I encourage you to reevaluate what you want to do in business.

An important key to returning the soul to business is learning to act in a responsible way and be accountable for our own actions. We cannot attribute our behavior to any external source. As creative and responsible adults, we are responsible for ourselves, and being accountable is up to us—accountable to every form of life, including the earth herself.

About ten years ago I had a dream that contained a verbal message and teaching. I was told that just as each individual has a power animal, couples, communities, and even countries have a power animal too. In America, for instance, the symbol is the eagle, and the bear represented the former Soviet Union.

Last year I worked with a spiritual organization that had lost its vision. I did a power animal retrieval for the group and taught the staff how to journey. By journeying to their power animal, they found guidance on creating a stronger partnership that could provide better service to their community. I knew the staff of this organization was not motivated by greed. They were coming from a "heart place," but they had lost their vision and needed some help regaining their focus and intention.

Shamanism is only one of many forms of spiritual practice. There are a number of ways to teach people in businesses to tap into Spirit. Because I work with shamanic journeying, that is the way my own vision unfolds. One reason I like working with shamanism is that the practice connects one with the earth and the cycles of nature, as well as all life forms. Any spiritual practice would be beneficial that could get our business community back in touch with the earth, back into a more natural way of life, and away from trying to have power over nature. The only prerequisite needed for doing this is that all the people involved work toward a similar goal: to provide service that does not compromise integrity, truth, and compassion.

As with personal healing, I advise against getting caught up with past mistakes and wounds. The business community must recognize its errors and then move on with the understanding that we have unlimited creative options now. The past is a road to the insights and understanding of the present. It is time to move forward now!

My hope is that we come out of this period understanding that material things are not more important than life itself; all life is sacred. I also hope we realize the importance of community and of sharing our abundance and skills for the good of the whole.

HEALING OUR COMMUNITIES

Change is happening everywhere around us. One place where we can see continual change is in our communities. Economic changes, political changes, earth changes—all in turn bring change in our communities. As people continually move in and out, there is a shift in the balance of ethnic groups. We see more people from foreign countries moving into our communities.

The change needed to create a positive future demands cooperation. We can no longer consider ourselves separate from our neighbors, whether they are in our own neighborhoods or in neighboring countries.

How can we foster this cooperation? We must learn how to live and work together, and we must welcome new people to our communities. Without this feeling of acceptance or welcome, there will always remain a sense of separation. I can see a time in the future when community rituals will be done to welcome newcomers and foster a sense of belonging and cooperation. The results would be mutual respect and a fostering of the desire to work in behalf of others.

One way to start this process is to organize neighborhood gatherings on a regular basis, seasonally or even monthly. Those who have been living longest in the community can welcome those who have just moved in, telling stories of what life is like in the area. There are endless stories of the eccentric people and unusual characteristics in every neighborhood I have ever lived in. This sense of community history gives us a feeling of the spirit of the place in which we live. What a wonderful way to develop a feeling of belonging, knowing that you are now becoming a part of the community's history! Be careful to organize around something positive—the tendency is to wait for a catastrophe to get organized, which only fosters negativity. This solution would not be hard to incorporate into our lives, and it would give all community members a sense of responsibility to one another and to the spirit of the community itself. I believe that would naturally foster a feeling of cooperation.

Amy writes:

> As I become more passionate about my own life, I develop more interest in my neighborhood, my community, and the world around me. Through caring for my own soul, I begin caring for the soul of the land, community, and the world. Shamanism has given me a deeper appreciation of our connection with all life and a new commitment to social responsibilities. I am now focusing on the ways in which I can be of service in the community.
>
> Having been a community organizer in years past, I am struck by the importance of spirituality in social change. Through journeying, I ask the spirits of the land for vision and guidance in serving my community. An important message is that the efforts of community groups are often fragmented and divided. We need to learn how to use our energy in a synergistic way to build relationships and energy. I began to talk with friends involved in environmental restoration projects about their current experiences in community work, about how each of us approaches our life's work with the help of the spirits. Through these discussions, the community of our efforts is unfolding and has become an important part of our relationships.
>
> A new challenge for Western culture is to realize our relationship to the community and to function as though we are a part of a larger circle. A spiritual approach to social responsibilities and change requires a shift in our thinking. I hold hope that through journeys and dialogue we can help restore soul and integrity to our communities.

RETRIEVING THE SOUL OF A PLACE

Shamanic belief holds that when a person experiences a trauma, a piece of that person's essence leaves the physical body in order to survive the experience. This is called soul loss, and it is the role of the shaman to retrieve that lost soul.

If we follow the principle of "as above, so below; as within, so without," the earth is a living being too. Thus when the earth experiences a trauma, she must lose a part of her soul. Some examples of abuse to the earth are bombing, clear-cutting, dumping of toxic waste products, nuclear testing, mining, and the constant excavation of land for structures, covering the earth with cement for our cities. Bringing back the soul of the entire earth would be overwhelming to an individual shamanic practitioner. But what we can do is bring back the soul of a place we have visited.

Perhaps you visit a place on the earth, and you have an intuitive feeling that this place has lost its soul. Or maybe you know that this particular location has suffered a trauma—a fire, a mass murder, a natural catastrophe, or any event that would cause destruction in the area. Because some natural occurrences that seem destructive can be healing to a piece of land, one has to get a sense of whether this land area has actually been hurt.

If you feel that the soul of a place has been lost due to trauma, is there anything that you can do for that piece of land? Consider doing a soul retrieval for that place. This method of soul retrieval is different from the one I describe in my book *Soul Retrieval*. In this situation ceremony can be very valuable in retrieving that lost life force.

As we progress through our own healing, we can more clearly recognize when we are in an area that suffers from soul loss. And as we heal further, we want the structures we live in and the earth we live on to be fully inspirited too.

I have asked participants in some of my workshops to journey for ceremonies to accomplish this healing. We have journeyed into the past to speak with ancestors about how to explore and deal with this issue. In doing my research for *Soul Retrieval*, I found that soul loss was the most common diagnosis of illness in shamanic communities. I also discovered that shamans worked to retrieve the soul of crops. Based on this information, I knew that shamans had to return the soul to pieces of land, so I decided to explore the ancient wisdom of our ancestors. There are endless ceremonies that have been brought back in my workshops. Again, I found that in doing this work, form is not important. The key is to have a strong intention and to come from a place of heart and love in creating the ceremony.

Doing this type of work raises an ethical issue. I would never do a soul retrieval on a piece of land that I consciously know is going to be abused again. There would be no purpose in doing that. For example, I would not do a soul retrieval on a nuclear test site where the testing would continue.

Doing such healing ceremonies raises the consciousness of our communities to the harm we actually do to the earth itself. Remember, it is not healthy to feel guilty or to lay blame around this damage. What is important is the realization that as an earth community, it is time for us to evolve and change our behavior.

In journeys to ancestors, we have discovered ceremonies to bring back the soul of a place.

Victoria wrote of her journey:

I was carried blindfolded in a travois by a warrior up a mountainside to a sacred spot. On the mountaintop where we arrived, there was a pole. I was met by warriors of the owl, eagle, bear, badger, and a few others, who formed a circle. I told them why I was there, and they opened their circle to allow a very old grandfather to pass through toward me. He was dressed in a large grayish white buffalo headdress with horns. The skin hung over his shoulders and down his back. He passed on this ritual to me.

Using a large turkey vulture feather, he began to sing back the spirit, raising the feather to the sky and drawing it down to the earth—as if drawing down the spirit. He told me I would know the song for the particular land I was working on—to sing the song for a while to begin to draw back the spirit.

"Then build a medicine circle with stone or whatever is available as a sacred focal point for the soul's return. Stand within the circle and continue singing and drawing down with the feather. Then go around the outside of the circle, drawing the spirit in and sealing it with the song and the feather.

"Then, singing, call back all the animals of that land.

"When completed, draw a cross across the circle to seal in the soul.

"Put corn and/or tobacco all around the outside of the circle.

"Then sit outside the circle and pray for the soul and ask whether there is something it needs or that you can do to help it."

When the return beat of the drum began, I was again blindfolded, put on the travois, and taken back down the side of the mountain.

Lois recalls that an ancestor spirit came to tell her of the following ritual:

Take up fine white cornmeal. Walk around the land sprinkling it with a spirit-calling whistle. Sprinkle and whistle. Then start rattling as you walk.

A song will come to you calling the soul back. Sing it as you walk and rattle. Call on the rain spirit and rain-calling helpers to come to this land. Call on the healing sun. Call on the ants to come. Call grass seeds to come. Call insects to come. Call birds to come.

Ask the spirits to help heal this land. Ask that all who come on this land will honor its healing. Call for the soul to come back to feel at home and to stay. Call for the web of life to return to this land.

All this will weave into the song you are to sing, as you rattle and walk the land. Do this again and again.

DCB describes her journey for the lost soul of land:

My power animal accompanies me to the Lower World. I hear a song:

> *Hoya . . . Hoya . . . Hoya*
> *Hey! Hey! Hey! Hey!*

I'm led to the mouth of a great and sacred cavern. There is a short man there, dressed in white plumes of feathers and fur. The whole cavern seems engulfed in soft white. The man has pitch black hair and sparkling eyes. He has a young, cherubic face with chubby cheeks and a ready smile. He is wise—very young, yet very wise. He stands straight with an air of dignity.

Others are there beating huge, round drums. One person has a long stick with a tight strand of animal hair to make a bow. On the top is the head of a dragonfly with outspread wings. The player has the bow in his hand and rubs his hands together while the bow, placed in the base of a gray stone with a hole in the top, makes a humming sound.

I am given two wooden handles with three white feathers sticking out of them and receive the following directions:

> *Envision the place of the land with lost soul,*
> *Circle three times to the left and face the sun,*
> *Circle three times to the right and face the sun,*
> *Using the strength of the land where you stand*
> *Take white feather handles*

Scoop the air in front of you,
Scoop three times.

Raise your feathers from earth to sun three times
And from sun to earth three times.
Bring your hands to your mouth
See soul as seed, tuck it under your tongue.

Now you will ride into the night
Ride your canoe through the stars
To the place of the land with the lost soul.

Glide through the night
Glide down to earth . . .

Step onto the earth,
Spit soul . . .
Twhoooo . . . twhoooo. Twhoooo . . . Twoooooh . . .
No water comes out . . . just soul
Spit it deep into the soil of earth.
Stomp it!

Earth drums beat fast . . .
now—
Hey! Hey! Hey-hey-hey

Circle wildly, stomping
Stomping!
Stomp three sets of four.
Changing directions.

Jump up and come down
Hands flat on the earth
Shout YA!

No sounds
In silence, soul is steady
Listening to see whether it is ready to stay,

Whether it is safe to stay . . .
To be welcomed home.

I would also like to include here two journeys that include rituals that can be used in urban areas.

In the first, Elaine journeyed to ask how she could do some healing work for the city in which she lives:

I journeyed to my power place in the Lower World and met my power animal. I stated that the intention of my journey was to find an ancestor from whom I could receive a ritual for healing a place. She told me that this was an Upper World journey and then flew me up.

There, I met my teacher and restated my intention. He took me to a woman who looked about sixty years old. Then there appeared an old man dressed in brown suede garments. I did not recognize these people, or ask who they were. Next I saw my maternal grandmother. I often work with a triad, and that was true on this journey as well. They agreed to speak to me in one voice.

I told them that I wanted a ritual for healing a place, specifically the city of Philadelphia. Furthermore, I was concerned with activating and accessing the positive energy that already existed there. They responded that many of the places in which flowers were planted are very soulful.

The ritual they described was something I could do on my own or with the assistance of like-minded people. We were to leave small offerings of honey for the bees around the city. In leaving these offerings, we were to ask the bees to carry a message to the flowers for assistance in healing the city. This request could simply be left in the honey. The request was that the flowers leave a veil of energized pollen across the city. This veil of pollen would then work to draw back the city's soul.

Additionally, I was instructed never to throw old, cut flowers directly into the trash, but rather to first leave them outside for a

day. I was also told that we could speak to the flowers directly
with our request.

At the end of the journey, after the drumming stopped, I
heard bees buzzing in my ears. For the first time in my life, I ex-
perienced this sound as that of my friends and allies.

Françoise shares this ritual:

Find a plant or tree, or plant one, or, if the place you are work-
ing with is a building, bring in a small plant or tree and put it
in a special spot. Gather rocks to form a circle around the plant.
Place four pointed crystals, or some other object that can serve
to transport soul parts, in each of the four directions. These ob-
jects should be inside the circle of stones with points toward the
plant. Sing, chant or breathe, or play an instrument into the
ground by the four crystals. The crystals transport the energy to
the plant, which becomes the opening, or vessel, for receiving
and distributing the soul. Call the soul of the place back with
strong intention. You may dance and sing to invite and welcome
back the soul.

The soul is then spread to the land through the roots, the
branches, and the leaves. As the tree breathes out its oxygen,
it will also release soul into the area around it. Leave the
crystals around the tree or plant until you can see or sense
that the soul is back into the place. It may take a few days or
weeks.

After we have been on a path of personal healing, it is time to
turn our attention outward and move from self-focus to a focus
on the community or world.

We need to change our business ethics and behavior from
money-oriented to service-oriented.

We need to change our business ethics to include the principle that all life is sacred and that life comes before money.

It is time to retrieve the soul of business:

- By trusting that if we provide a needed service, we will get the needed exchange for that service

- By inspiriting business with integrity and compassion

- By expanding our concept of partnership and seeing ourselves work together for the good of the whole

- By bringing spirituality into business, concentrating on the spiritual and natural path, and not using Spirit for the goal of amassing material gain.

We must be responsible and accountable for our actions.

We cannot get stuck in past mistakes or get lost in issues of guilt and blame. We must evolve and move forward.

In order to create a positive future we need to foster cooperation.

It is important for members of communities to feel a sense of belonging in order to foster a desire for cooperation.

Just as an individual can lose a part of the soul, so can a place on the earth lose its soul.

A ceremony can be performed to return the soul of a piece of land.

Ethically, it is best to do this ceremony for a place that, to your best knowledge, will not be abused again.

Thoughts to ponder:

> *What we give, we receive. When we focus our energy on the good of all life and concentrate on using our energy as creatively as possible, the natural law is for our physical, emotional, and spiritual needs to be met.*

When we think of a business, we should be able to describe it using the words integrity *and* compassion.

EXERCISES

The task of bringing soul back into business is a big one, so please be gentle with yourself. Remember, you need to make only those changes that are not overwhelming for you at this time.

1. We are all involved in business of some kind. How much of your time do you devote to thinking about money?

How much time do you devote to being creative?

How can you balance these two aspects of your life?

2. Do you feel you are partners with your employer and co-workers?

What would you need to deepen your partnership? Use your imagination and stay positive, even if you think this type of partnership is not possible.

3. What kind of work would be meaningful for you; what kind of work would you feel passionate about participating in?

4. How do you feel you can better serve your community?

5. Find some neighbors that you can create a small gathering with. Have a "block party." Share any stories you know of the history of your neighborhood. Talk about your hopes and visions for your community. Brainstorm on how you can cooperate with one another to improve the quality of life in your community.

6. Think of a place in nature you go to visit that you feel might have lost its soul or life force. Create a ceremony that you can do alone or with others to call the life force back to that place again.

7. Create a sacred space in your house so you know what it feels like to be in a place that has soul. To do this, put objects that are meaningful to you in your room. Use objects that are full of life. You might use fresh flowers or objects from nature that call to you.

CHAPTER 8

WORKING
WITH
THE CYCLES
OF NATURE

We are part of nature. We do not exist separately from the natural world. One of the outcomes of modern technology is the ability to set up an artificial world that has moved us away from what the rest of nature is doing.

If we see nature as a mirror for our own process, we must look at the message given to us. Weather patterns have become extremely violent. Many communities experience greater problems with insect blights and diseases caused by insects. In chapter 2 I talk about needing passion for life. I wonder if the earth as a living organism has more passion for life than we humans do. I wonder how our lives would change if we were willing to look at the process of evolution occurring naturally on our planet today.

For example, let's think about fire and its effects. The human experience is often of the loss that comes from fire. But what happens in nature after a fire? Fire allows certain seeds to germinate and grow. There is also a purifying quality that comes with floods and hurricanes. In shifting our awareness to natural cycles, we can begin to understand that although with a "natural disaster" there will be loss, there is also, on another level, evolution, growth, and healing being attended to by the earth and other forms of life.

To understand creativity, we must look at nature. What are other life forms doing in spring, summer, fall, and winter? Do we make life harder on ourselves because we are so "out of sync" with nature? In life after healing, we must look at ways that we can be part of nature, instead of living with the illusion that we have power over nature.

When I had a private practice in counseling psychology, I noticed that in September I heard a common complaint among my clients. Often people would come into a session complaining that they felt as though they were dying. I instructed anyone with this complaint at this time of year to look out the window and see what was happening to the trees. This process occurs in all climates, whether or not we can see it. In the fall a natural process of death occurs, and it is a time to "let go." At this point in my work I started to realize how much our technological society has removed us from nature.

A couple of years ago Isis advised me to follow the laws of nature and move away from human laws. Part of my path has been to understand her instructions. I learned that scarcity does not exist in nature, that it is a human concept. Nature's cycles might include a period of dormancy, such as winter, but there is no scarcity.

I can draw an example of this from my own writing. When I wrote my first book, *Soul Retrieval: Mending the Fragmented Self,* I found that weeks would go by when I had nothing to write. On the outside, one could view this as a frustrating time when I was blocked. But I intuitively knew that it was during these weeks when no words formed on paper that the most important work was happening. For something was occurring internally. Thoughts and information were churning, and my own process was percolating. I never forced myself to write during these times, for I knew what was truly going on. I did not think consciously about my internal process; I just allowed it to happen, knowing and trusting that when I was ready to say something, the words would come naturally. I was not disappointed in this intuition, for when I was ready to write, I found that my words flowed effortlessly.

In nature's seasons we can observe different processes. There is the time for readying the soil and for preparing and planting the seeds. There is the time to nurture the soil and the seeds we have planted, and the growing season, when we see the flowers and fruits of our labor. And there is the harvest. Finally there is dormancy, when the earth rests. We can see these times literally in nature and symbolically in our lives. All projects that we create— even our own lives and bodies—follow these processes.

The seasons are only one aspect of nature. Think of water. Our bodies are mostly made of water. Once, when I was writing my first book, I was taking a shamanic journey to become the ocean, to see what I could learn by merging with such a great natural force. The ocean reminded me about tides and gave me this message: "Just as there are seasons to a project, you must also remember the tides. There is a time to actively put your project out into the world, and there is also a time to retreat to gather energy and power."

The moon also has a great influence on cycles. One day when I was visiting with Isis in a journey, she said that she wanted me to meet a new teacher. I was intrigued and mystified, wondering what she had in mind. She took me to the moon. I had wanted to understand the phases of the moon better, but no matter how many books I read or moon calendars I studied, I simply could not get a feeling about what any of the information meant. The moon herself instructed me. Where I could not visually understand what moon calendars were trying to depict about the moon phases, the moon showed me herself. She said, "Watch how I wax and how I wane. Watch how I grow into my fullness and how I move into darkness."

She showed her movement to me several times until I could feel my own body waxing and waning with her, following her phases and truly feeling what she was experiencing. I finally understood what I had been trying to learn, experientially and through the written word. I was able to follow the amazing flow of the moon's cycle.

She also explained how and when to plant in my garden: As she moves from new to full, she sends energy into the plant stem, fruit, and flowers. This is the time to plant crops that flower and produce above ground. When she wanes, she magnetically draws energy from the plant into the root, a good time to plant root crops because her energy is more available to them.

The moon said that she wanted me to start living my life according to her phases. She said, "Be active, and create new things when I am going from new to full. Become inactive and let yourself rest and regenerate, allow your process to be internal, when I am going from full to new. Pull your energy back just as a wave is pulled back as the tide goes out."

At first I was very excited about this new assignment, and I felt honored to have the moon as a teacher in my life. Then my practical side kicked in. My work schedule was not set up for this kind of cycle. I had a hard time orienting my life to this new way of being, scheduling when it was time for me to be outwardly creative and when it was time for me to turn inside myself. I journeyed back to the moon and apologized for not acting on what she had taught me. She responded, "What I shared with you was for your benefit and learning. I am not going anywhere. When it is time for you to follow my teaching and learn from me, I will still be here."

She was right. The artificial structure that I had set up in my life caused consequences for me that I had to endure. The process of activity and regeneration is a natural one, and when I continued to go against that natural process, I had to pay the price. Living in this unnatural way caused undue stress on my psyche and my body. I could easily have become overwhelmed by all this;

however, because I am so clear in my own life and in teaching others that we have to make changes step by step, I was able to stay centered. So I did not change my process overnight, but I started where I could—in my garden.

My moon journey was in April before it was time for me to plant my garden. I bought a *Farmer's Almanac* so that I did not have to "reinvent the wheel" with gardening. I was open to learning from those who had gone before me. My goal was to look up at the night sky and know what to plant, but I had to be realistic about my starting place. I was brought up in Brooklyn, an urban environment where what was happening in the night sky seemed inconsequential. Although I knew many of my students and peers were far ahead of me in the ordinary realms of understanding nature, I had to honor my process and personal evolution. I had to acknowledge my own lack of understanding of nature and start from the beginning. I am still in process with this, but I have become tremendously aware of what is happening around me day and night.

More importantly, I also have become more conscious of my feelings as the natural world changes around me hourly, daily, and seasonally. For example, I have learned that summer is not my best season. It is not a time for me to be active and creative. Instead I feel extremely vulnerable, so I need to create an abundance of time alone.

During fall and winter I am in heaven. I can be out and about, creative and social. These are times when I feel strong and in my own power. It took me years to learn this about myself, but I realize now that honoring my own process means scheduling myself according to my own natural cycle.

Often we get caught up in what we are told is natural instead of following our own rhythms. What is our own inherent rhythm? What are the best times for us seasonally? What are the best times to retreat and regenerate? What are the best times of the day for us to be creative and energetic? When do we need to get rest, and how much rest do we need? These questions are important to our lives after healing. The answers vary among individuals; no one can answer for you. To be the most creative individual possible, each of us must get in touch with his or her own cycles, seasons, and times of day that are most productive.

Because we live in a society ruled by linear time, trying to live on our own time creates a challenge. We are taught to serve the clock and not our own cycles. But remember, we have to start somewhere, by becoming aware that we have removed ourselves from the natural world, then teaching others what we have learned. Begin making changes in your life where it is possible to be flexible. Use this information to change how you construct your free time.

We can learn a tremendous amount from nature, and the best ways to do it are to be more observant of the natural world and to be open to receiving direct revelation from nature. For example, I talk to different aspects of nature. In shamanism we can communicate with nature spirits by taking a shamanic journey outside time and space to learn from them. But there are other ways to gain access to the same information. We can use the method of direct revelation—just shifting our perception to see and hear our natural world in other ways.

Go outside and sit with some life form in nature that you might like to learn from—a tree, a flower, a pond, a turtle— whatever feels right for you. Next, get centered and grounded. The easiest way to do this is by breathing slowly and deeply and experiencing yourself as clearly as you can in your surroundings. Take a moment and feel the air on your skin. What is the temperature? Is it warm or cool? Is it wet or dry? Is the air still, or can you feel a breeze? With your eyes closed, listen to the sounds around you and open yourself to receive all the smells. Remember the concept of receiving that you read about in chapter 2. Open yourself to receive with all your physical senses. Now have the intention to open and receive with all your invisible senses—the invisible sense of sight, sound, and feeling that might come as an intuition or a knowing. When you feel centered and, perhaps, in a slightly altered state, you are ready to learn.

Have you ever been out in nature taking a walk when you feel an "opening"? This deep connection with the natural world puts you in tune with a different cycle from the linear one we experience in our daily routine. It creates a shift in perception that might make you feel a bit altered, maybe even euphoric. You probably have experienced the peace that taking a walk in nature can provide. If you haven't had this experience, then make sure you create it for yourself. Just find a park to walk in. To create a better life for yourself you must be able to set aside the time and space to connect with the natural world. This is a "must" if you really want to create a positive future, for we can no longer afford to live so separated from nature.

Once you have opened a space in your life to spend some time in nature, pick one life form that you would like to learn from. It can be an element like the earth, water, air, or fire, or it can be some other inhabitant of the earth like a rock, tree, plant, bird, insect, or leaf. Indigenous people knew how to do this and learned to work with plants for healing. They talked to the plants. Most of us have lost this ability because we have let the senses needed to do this work lie dormant. It's never too late to exercise and develop these senses again, but I ask you to start small. First just learn how to communicate with other life forms without jumping too far into healing work. Remember that most of us have been out of touch for many generations, and be patient with the learning process.

A few years ago I had a wonderful conversation with a tree. It was fall, and I was in upstate New York, teaching a workshop on speaking to the spirits of nature. I instructed all the participants to find a tree that they could sit with and get some information on what they needed to learn from the season of fall. I decided to participate in the exercise also. I went to sit with an oak tree that was in the peak of fall color. I asked permission of the tree to just sit with it for a while. One just "knows" when permission is being granted or when a life form doesn't want to be disturbed; I felt I received permission to sit with the tree. I allowed myself to lean back into the tree and into the earth beneath me. The air was fresh and crisp, and it was starting to get a little cold. I sat and breathed deeply, allowing myself to merge with the energy of the tree and leaving behind my thoughts of physical comfort. As I sat, I asked the tree if it had a message for me. In my mind I heard a message:

"You know the difference between you and me?" asked the tree.

"No," I responded with a feeling of curiosity.

"You sit and think about what it is time to let go of in your life. Now it is time to let go of this belief, or that attitude, or this feeling. I don't do that. My leaves just drop to the ground naturally. I don't sit and think that now I'm going to drop my bottom right leaf. I wonder what would happen to your life if you allowed what you needed to let go of in this fall season to fall away naturally without actively deciding what should be released and how it should be released?"

I felt a little surprised by what I was hearing. I detected an attitude in what the tree was sharing with me, and I didn't expect to sit with a tree with an attitude. But the tree was absolutely correct. I had been too focused on becoming active in my transformation process and was completely out of balance, not letting things unfold naturally in my life. Although my time with the tree was a humbling experience, it was definitely the most important teaching I received that year, and it took me quite a while to integrate that message into my being and into my life.

There is a balance in nature. As humans, each of us is challenged to learn when it is time to be active, plant seeds, and nurture them and when it is time to allow the plant to grow and die naturally. This metaphor relates to all projects, all relationships, and the different natural phases in our lives.

How do we learn this process? The first step is slowing down our lives. We get into a too-quick rhythm that is often dysfunctional. Instead, we need to slow down to our natural rhythm. This takes a commitment of time and an increased awareness of what is needed in our own lives and by our own bodies, minds, and spirits to create and maintain a state of harmony and health.

We must look at how the rest of nature is affected by the movement of sun, moon, and stars and how our own natural rhythm fits in with this. Slow down and be more observant of the world around you. Tune into your feelings and level of energy and see how they relate to the different cycles, tides, and currents. Notice when you feel filled with power and energy, or when you feel the most vulnerable, needing to retreat, to pull your energy back for a while. Think about the currents in the ocean: See and feel your own body bringing waves of energy and emotion crashing to the surface, then pulling them back.

Your level of creativity will increase manyfold as you become a part of the sun, moon, earth, and stars again, for you will be working with the flow of life. I believe this should be the ultimate goal for all people who say they want to create a positive future, to work for the highest good of all life.

We are part of nature, not separate from the natural world.

Modern technology has allowed us to live in artificial cycles.

Nature is a mirror for our own behavior.

Natural disasters are really a process of growth, evolution, and healing.

Nature has its own inherent cycles, represented by the seasons and the cycles of the sun, moon, and stars.

As part of nature we are affected by its seasons and cycles. We can look at our own projects and see how they fit into the natural process (preparing and planting the seed, nurturing the soil by composting and aerating, watching the growth and flowering, enjoying the fruits of our labors, experiencing the end of the project, experiencing a period of dormancy). We can notice the currents and know when to put our project out in the world and when to pull back to regather energy.

It is time for us to return to the laws of nature.

We need to tune into our own natural rhythms. To be creative, we must get in touch with our own cycles, seasons, and times of day when we are most productive.

We are currently a society ruled by linear time.

To learn from nature we must be more observant. We can also get messages through direct revelation.

Take time for yourself to be out in nature.

Slow down and notice what you need to do to be attuned to a more natural cycle in your life. Observe what is happening in the natural world around you.

Thought to ponder:

> *It takes a lot of water to bear good fruit.*

EXERCISES

1. Raise your awareness of times of the day. Look at and acknowledge the best times of day for you to be creative. Write a few sentences for yourself about this.

2. How are you affected by the light outside? Make a list of how your moods and feelings change with the quality of the light.

3. What are your favorite seasons? Write a story or poem about them and why they are your favorites.

4. Write about how your moods, creativity, and energy are affected by the different seasons.

5. Go outside at night and notice the sky. Find the moon and keep a journal about how you feel during the different phases of the moon.

6. Following the instructions at the end of the chapter, create time for yourself to speak to the elements and other life forms in nature. Keep a journal about what you learn from doing this.

CHAPTER 9

THE DOORWAY IS THROUGH THE HEART

Song of Return
(Soul Retrieval Poem)

An ageless shaman sped through the universe
found me wandering and brought me home.
With the wind of her breath, she blew in my
impish, dizzying, wise little young one and
as we met, sang "welcome home"
the road's been different ever since
. . . full of changing colours . . .
So gathered up, I now can fly
. . . over meadows
. . . down long grassy hills.
And soaring great circles
wild things surround me
together together
humming Love's praise.

—Carol Proudfoot-Edgar

Siempre crawled into bed. She turned toward her window one last time to take a look at the night before she drifted into sleep. The sky was black, and she could see just the sliver of a new moon. She sank down under the covers, feeling the softness and warmth beneath her enhancing her drowsiness. She closed her eyes and was instantly pulled deep inside herself. In her dream state she met with Isis, who was waiting for her in the deep state of being one would call the void, the place of darkness before creation began.

"You do realize, Siempre, that you live in a territory of illusion, don't you?" Isis asks.

Siempre's dreaming free soul responds, "Yes, I have always understood that."

Isis continues, "The territory of illusion guards the territory of reality. One cannot get to this place before one's time."

Siempre nods as if she understands Isis's words. She understands on a level that cannot be explained by words; it is a felt sense of knowing.

"I've felt for some time now, Isis, that shamans knew how to access this reality. It seems to me that there is a place somewhere behind the dimension of illusion that I live in where perfection still exists. To me, the world of nonordinary reality that

*I have been journeying to is the world of Spirit. I believe there is
another territory that I have not gained access to yet, and it
can't be found through journeying. It's a place where there is no
disease or pollution, for they have not been created there. I know
inside myself that shamans knew how to get to this place. They
knew how to bring that perfection through to this reality. They
truly knew how to transmute energy, for they understood what
was real and what was illusion. I have nothing to back this up.
I just know it in my heart."*

*"You are on the right track, Siempre," Isis replies. "But I can-
not help you find the place you are looking for. It will take a
shift of perception on your part, and you must find the path on
your own."*

"Can you give me any clues about where to start, Isis?"

*"You will find the door you are looking for in the garden,
Siempre. That's why I have been encouraging you to fully experience nature. You must get away from human laws and return to
the laws of nature. Human laws and the laws of linear time
keep you stuck in the territory of illusion. Return to the way of
nature, and what is true and real will be shown to you. In the
garden you will find that the plants growing are true life. They
are not an illusion. Find your way back to the garden, and you
will find the reality you are looking for.*

*"Siempre, there is one more piece of information I will share
with you now. It is time for you to start working with your oversoul."*

*Siempre was taken aback. She had never heard any of her
helping spirits use this term with her. She knew this term from
the writings of others but didn't know what it meant. She did
not know what Isis was referring to but decided to let Isis finish
before interrupting her with questions.*

*When she felt that Siempre's attention was again focused on
her words, Isis continued, "You can do for yourself what your
power animals and teachers in nonordinary reality have been*

doing for you in your lifetime. The part of yourself that acts as we do is called the oversoul. This is the part of yourself that acts on your behalf as we have been doing for you. It is time for your helping spirits to slowly start removing support from you. Please do not fear. You have done nothing wrong. It is just time for you to move to the next level in your own evolution. We will with-draw from your life slowly. We will not desert you. Just realize it is time for us—and you—to move on now. And, please, always remember that you are truly loved by the Universe and all your helping spirits."

Siempre found herself drifting in these last words of Isis. She was aware that Isis was no longer with her and that she was alone in a deep stillness where there was no time or life. She had no idea how long she remained in this state. At some point, the morning sun shining in Siempre's face awoke her from this deep place she had traveled to. She awoke slowly with the awareness that she felt full from the night.

Siempre followed Isis's advice and began to spend more time in the garden. Her life was full, and change did not come over-night. But she was committed to her path. One day as Siempre was sitting in the garden, admiring the vibrant colors surround-ing her, she heard an almost inaudible voice that said to her, "The doorway you are looking for is through your heart."

This is where Siempre's story leaves off and where my own story continues. I am still looking for the doorway, and I know it is close. There is still a lot for me to learn on my Spirit path in this lifetime. From what I have learned and from what I have experi-enced, I am sure of one thing: What we see, touch, smell, and feel is our creation. It has been part of our evolution to experience suffering—possibly to learn about compassion. Do we need to move on now to another level of our evolution? Must we change our creation? Can we once again experience the beauty of life and nature? Is it time now to return to the natural flow of all life?

I am not saying that such a life brings only pleasure. Not only does all life experience the beauty and warmth of nature's cycles and currents, it also endures the changes that sometimes seem hard to our human souls. But we can achieve balance.

Let's find the place inside ourselves that gives us the courage and strength to take responsibility for our lives. If this world truly is the territory of illusion and we have come here to learn about manifestation, then let's create a good story for ourselves and for all of life.

The first step is to change our behavior toward ourselves and to the rest of life on the planet. The next step is to find the doorway through our hearts. Once we pass through, who knows what is possible?

It is possible to find a reality where we can bring perfection to this dimension. We can learn to transmute and transform energy.

First, we must learn to be compassionate for all life and to be responsible for our behavior and our creations. We must change our current behavior to support life. For as we heal ourselves and the planet, we don't want to re-create abuse.

The doorway is through the heart.

Thoughts to ponder:

Love heals.

The future is created by our present; stay in the present.

Live your gift.

EXERCISE

1. Experience your life as an art form. Pick the art form that you would enjoy working with, whether it be a painting, a sculpture, a story, a piece of music, or something else.

Stand back a few feet from the art form you have created. How would you change your creation? Remember that the creation of all art requires time and nurturance and that all art is never truly completed. It is always in process.

AFTERWORD

THE STORY
OF SIEMPRE

About two years ago, I woke at dawn, with a start. I felt that I must immediately get up to write. This is unusual behavior for me, for I tend to be a late sleeper whenever I can have the luxury of time.

I went to my desk and began to write what was filling my head. What came out is what you were reading when you began chapter 1. There is a fascinating synchronicity in this story.

After I wrote that page I did not write again until two years later when I began to write *Welcome Home: Following Your Soul's Journey Home*. When I wrote that first page, I did not know where the name Siempre came from. But her name came to me strongly. A year after writing about her, I began to hear my teacher Isis start to teach me about the concept of eternity. After Isis shared her message about the importance of this concept, I found out that *siempre* in Spanish means "always."

I will always wonder if Isis knew that I would be writing a new book on the future, asking us to remember the eternity of all life.

APPENDIX

SHAMANISM

Shamanism is a way of accessing spiritual guidance that dates back tens of thousands of years. It is practiced all over the world, in Siberia, Lapland, parts of Asia, Africa, Australia, and North and South America. *Shaman* is a Tungus word meaning "healer" or "one who sees in the dark." The Tungus people live in Siberia and Mongolia.

A shaman is a man or woman who enters an altered state of consciousness and travels outside time and space into nonordinary reality, which I think of as a universe parallel to ours.

Shamans use some form of percussion, usually a drum, to access nonordinary reality. Scientists investigating why so many people around the world use drums found that listening to a monotonous drumbeat changes the brain waves from a beta state (when we are engaged in normal activity) to a theta state (like that of deep meditation). The drum allows the shaman to leave the body behind and travel into this parallel universe. I think of the drum as the path out of and back into the body.

In nonordinary reality a shaman can meet spirit helpers that appear as animals or teachers in human form. The shaman also can ask for healing help or divine information.

Three territories exist in nonordinary reality: the Lower World, the Middle World, and the Upper World. These regions are distinguished by different characteristics determined by the particular shaman journeying. For me, for example, the Lower World is very earthy. I can feel the landscape around me and stick my fingers into the earth. I might experience a forest, a desert, large bodies of water, or caves with crystals in them. I usually see terrains that are similar to places in nature that I associate with spots on the planet. The Upper World is more ethereal. I "know" what I am standing on, but I am not sure exactly what it is. The colors are brighter and more pastel than those of the Lower World.

Both the Lower and the Upper worlds have many levels. We live in an unlimited universe; therefore, the territories are endless.

In nonordinary reality, the Middle World comes closest to our ordinary reality. Here I see scenes that I would experience in my waking life, but I am in an altered state of consciousness when looking at them. I will see buildings, cars, and people, but I will be outside time. Shamans usually travel to the Middle World to find lost and stolen objects. I also travel to the Middle World to speak to the spirit of a client who is in a coma or unconscious to get permission to do healing work on his or her behalf.

Most shamanic cultures around the world believe that when we are born, the spirit of an animal takes pity on us and volunteers to protect us and keep us healthy and safe. This animal is called a power animal. Most of us have two to three power animals around us at one time, although some people report having whole zoos of power animals.

The beauty of shamanism is that a person's experience is neither right nor wrong. Therefore, each person on a shamanic path learns to trust his or her own experience and not to follow any rules or doctrines. The only doctrine of shamanism is that this work be used to benefit all life and for the purpose of healing. But there are no rules about how many spirit helpers one can have, or what the Upper and Lower Worlds look like.

Typically, a shaman is a person who is called to a healing path. A shaman's role is to heal both the living and the dead.

The shamanic framework involves three main causes of illness. Shamanism views emotional and physical illness as the same. A shaman works with helping spirits and does not use his or her own inherent energy or form a personal opinion on how the work should proceed. To find the correct diagnosis of the illness, the shaman journeys to the power animal or teacher who works in a healing capacity to ask about the spiritual cause of the illness and the appropriate spiritual healing technique. It is important to remember that shamans work with the spiritual aspect of illness; this healing can be used in conjunction with psychological, physical, and medical modalities.

Typically, in traveling to nonordinary reality to consult with helping spirits, a shaman may discover one or more of three possible causes of illness. First, a person's power animal may leave without a new one taking its place. Certain symptoms are associated with power loss. In this case, a person might suffer from chronic illness such as colds, viruses, or flus; such a person cannot seem to protect the body's integrity. Chronic depression or suicidal tendencies are other possibilities. Another symptom of power loss would be persistent misfortune; for example, someone is robbed, falls down the stairs, and then loses a job. One wonders whether this individual has been jinxed. From a shamanic perspective, this person has lost his or her power. In a case of power loss, the shaman journeys into nonordinary reality to find an animal who is willing to come back with the shaman to restore power to the client.

Another cause of illness might be soul loss. The soul is our life force, our essence, our vitality. When one suffers an emotional or physical trauma, a piece of that essence separates from the body and travels into nonordinary reality to survive the experience. The psychological term for this is *dissociation.* One difference between shamanism and psychology is that psychology does not address where these parts go when they dissociate. Through shamanic journeying, we find them in either the Lower World, the Upper World, or the Middle World, living outside time.

In a shamanic society, when a person suffers a trauma (for example, a hunting accident), the community immediately comes together, and the shaman performs a soul retrieval with the support of that community. Because in our culture we no longer consider the spiritual form of illness, shamanic practitioners today have more challenges in doing soul retrievals. We might have to go back ten, twenty, even forty years or more, looking for the soul and why it left.

Some causes of soul loss include incest, emotional and/or physical abuse, accidents, surgery, wartime stress, illness, divorce, or the death of a loved one. Anything that is seen as traumatic is liable to result in soul loss. For example, if I was going to be in a head-on auto accident, the very last place I would want to be is in my body. It is very important to understand that soul loss is a survival mechanism and occurs because the person's psyche or being could not survive the pain of the experience while remaining fully present in the body. Not uncommonly, I hear incest survivors report that they were looking down on their bodies while the trauma occurred.

There are many signs that indicate soul loss. If a person dissociates, most likely there will be soul loss. Some people report that they have been observing life like a movie instead of fully experiencing it. A person might feel as if he or she never came back from the anesthesia after surgery, or may still feel "spaced out" after an accident. Sometimes people lose a piece of their soul to a lost relationship or to a person who has died. Soul loss prevents people from moving forward with life; they are always psychically connected to an old relationship, always looking backward or projecting loss into the future.

As with loss of personal power, chronic illness is an indicator of soul loss. The Universe cannot stand a void, so when someone is not fully in his or her body, an illness might enter to fill the space. Likewise, a person may demonstrate soul loss through addictive behavior, by using food, alcohol, drugs, relationships, work, or money to fill the empty hole or void left by the wandering soul. Chronic depression and suicidal tendencies might also be signs of soul loss, as they were for power loss. Soul loss leaves us feeling fragmented, making it hard to connect with others and life around us. This feeling of disconnection can result in depression.

Coma is also a form of soul loss. In this case a person experiences soul loss so severe that a large chunk of his or her being goes out of the body and the body becomes unconscious. When we lose our whole soul, we die.

Whenever someone tells me, "I have never been the same since . . . ," or "I don't feel whole," or "I don't feel all here," I suspect soul loss. In itself, soul loss is good because it enables an individual to survive a traumatic experience. From a shamanic perspective, the problem occurs when the soul does not come back on its own. It may be lost in nonordinary reality, not knowing how to return to the body, or it may not want to come back, especially when the person has been abused. Here the shamanic practitioner must negotiate with the soul, letting it know how life has changed and that the trauma is in the past.

Finally, a soul might not come back on its own because it has been stolen by another person. This phenomenon is more common than one might think. In shamanic cultures soul stealing may have been a form of psychic warfare. No bombs are dropped; instead, souls are stolen. In our culture, I frequently see soul stealing but it is usually done on an unconscious level. Incest survivors often say, "My father stole my soul." Sometimes I hear, "My lover stole my soul." How many country and western musicians sing about having their souls or hearts stolen?

Why steal someone's soul? There are a variety of reasons. Maybe someone is jealous of another's power. Perhaps a person is desperate for energy and sees an energetic child or adult from whom to draw energy. In a divorce or separation, even with the death of a loved one, soul stealing maintains some connection. Of course, the reverse process occurs when a child or adult gives away a piece of soul.

One of the points I feel people need to be educated about is that you cannot steal another's power or energy and use it for yourself. What ends up happening is that you weaken the person whose soul you have stolen and you become burdened by unusable energy. It ends up being a lose-lose situation for all concerned. Moreover, another person cannot steal your soul unless you let them. As a child you might not have had the strength or the know-how to resist. As adults we all have the choice to leave a situation or resist.

When I feel that someone is trying to steal my soul, I either call my power animal to me for protection or visualize myself sitting in a translucent blue egg. The blue egg visualization is a method a Chumash medicine woman taught me years ago for protection. If I feel that I have stolen another person's soul, I perform a very simple ritual to give it back. For example, I might intentionally send back the soul of a person on smoke of incense or a fire. I might blow the piece of soul into a crystal or stone and give this object to the person as a gift. I can also just ask my helping spirits to take the soul to whom it belongs. I might give a person whose soul I've stolen a gift representing the soul piece I took. The power of ritual is intention; it doesn't matter what form it takes.

When a soul leaves the body, it might go to the Lower World, the Upper World, or the Middle World. In speaking about soul loss I am talking about partial soul loss. Again if the whole soul leaves, we die. In doing a soul retrieval I might see parts that left as a child due to trauma, and parts as a teenager, as well as parts of ourselves as adults. I see the souls as the age they left. So I might see a newborn, or a three-year-old, or a thirteen-year-old, or a twenty-seven-year-old.

One of the basic premises of shamanic healing is that another person intervenes in the spiritual realms on the client's behalf. In the case of soul loss, it is the role of the shamanic practitioner to journey on behalf of the client, locate the soul parts with the aid of helping spirits, negotiate for their return, and "blow" them back into the client's body. This is a very advanced shamanic technique and should never be attempted without the appropriate training.

Lacking personal power or losing soul parts leaves an opening for a spiritual intrusion to enter. If a person comes to me complaining of localized pain or illness such as cancer, a heart problem, a neck problem, or stomach disorders, I suspect that this person suffers from a spiritual intrusion. When I journey for a person with such a complaint, I might see something that obviously should not be in the person's body, something that I have a strong emotional response to. For example, I might see a threatening fanged reptile or swarms of insects or black sludge. These intrusions are not evil; they are just misplaced. With spiritual intrusions the shaman pulls or sucks out the intrusion and places it back in nature where it can do no harm. Usually the intrusions are transmuted into a large body of water, where its power can be neutralized.

Spiritual intrusions are caused by negative thought forms. They can be sent consciously or unconsciously by another, they can be picked up walking down any populated city street, or they can be formed inside oneself if problematic feelings remain unexpressed and unresolved. I speak about this issue in chapters 3 and 4.

SUMMARY

In looking at the spiritual cause of emotional and/or physical illness, a shaman journeys to her power animal or teacher and discovers whether a client is suffering from power loss, soul loss, or a spiritual intrusion. Usually it is a combination of these, if not all of them. It is the role of the shaman, through the assistance of helping spirits, to perform the appropriate healing.

Because shamanism works with the spiritual aspect of illness, we do not know what the result will be on the physical level. Clients might find relief of symptoms through the shamanic healing, or they might need to augment the healing with assistance from a counselor, psychologist, medical doctor, herbalist, acupuncturist, body worker, or a healer from some other tradition. The self-healing aspect of the work occurs as clients look at what changes they need to make in life to maintain their health.

A shaman is also a psychopomp, a conductor of souls. In this role the shaman helps the deceased. In a sudden or traumatic death such as in an auto accident or a train or plane crash, or murder or suicide, a person may not have made a smooth transition from the Middle World to the Upper World. In such a case, the shaman's role is to lead the lost soul from the place where it is stuck, to the light, where it can heal and evolve.

A person pursuing a shamanic path can use shamanism in another way besides healing. The shamanic journey can also be used to divine information. It is possible to journey, for yourself or for another person, to a power animal or teacher to ask a question. The shaman journeys to nonordinary reality to access information, so journeying can also be used to access spiritual guidance in one's own life.

If you want to read more about the information provided in this appendix, I recommend *The Way of the Shaman*, by Michael Harner, and my book *Soul Retrieval: Mending the Fragmented Self.*

ACKNOWLEDGMENTS

I gratefully acknowledge all those who helped me bring *Welcome Home: Following Your Soul's Journey Home* into the world.

I thank Cynthia Bechtel for her work in editing and Polly Rose for typing the manuscript. I especially want to thank both these wonderful women for the constant support and encouragement they provided during my writing. I also want to thank Jim Hill for his help in getting my project started and Debbie Doyle for her clerical help. I also honor Jaye Oliver for her wonderful illustrations. It was great fun working with her. I thank Phil Welch for photographing me.

I am grateful to Barbara Moulton, my editor at Harper San Francisco, for her friendship and guidance during the writing of my book, and for believing in me and my project. All the people of Harper San Francisco have been a delight to work with and have helped me have faith in how a business can have a soul.

I am especially grateful to my clients and all the people who have studied shamanism with me who confirmed that *Welcome Home: Following Your Soul's Journey Home* was a much-needed book and supported me in putting out my message. There were many who sent written contributions to the book, and I thank all of you for your generosity of time and energy. Whether your work appears here or not, I thank you. I thank Linda Crane, Harriet Toben, and Carol Proudfoot Edgar for the poems they contributed.

I want to acknowledge Michael Harner, who has been a wonderful friend and teacher and partner in my work. I support him totally in his work as he has always supported me.

The love and encouragement of many friends and family members added a great deal of power and energy to my work. I especially thank my partner, Easy Hill, and my parents, Aaron and Lee Ingerman. I would like to thank and honor Ray Swartley for reminding me about eternity. I thank Woods for welcoming me home.

Most of all I want to thank and honor my power animals and teachers in nonordinary reality for their continual love and teachings. It was a real honor for me to bring through some of Isis's messages; I am grateful for all her teachings. My power animal provides a constant source of love and power, and I never feel alone knowing he and Isis are with me. There are many invisible helpers that also lend their power and wisdom, and I thank and honor them for that.

I give thanks for my life.

INDEX

Creativity: choosing focus for, 35, 84–88, 101; exercises, 102, 158–59, 167; Isis's version of, 14, 17; self-awareness of, 157
Cycles, natural, 150–54

Dancing, in releasing rituals, 90, 93, 94–95, 98
Death: in natural cycles, 150; shamanic guidance after, 178; as soul loss, 175; as transition, 17, 30, 34–35
Dissociation. *See* Soul loss
Dormancy, in natural cycles, 150–51
Dreams: exercises, 37, 125; healing, 29, 115–17; teaching, 5, 28; vs. journeying, 69–70
Drumming: in journeying, 13, 25, 42–43, 60, 70, 171; in rituals, 96–97, 98

Earth: abuse of, 129–30, 136–42; and thought energy, 42–43
Ego, 108–9; exercises, 124; information from, 110, 111
Empathy, 59–61, 122
Energy: changing focus of, 99–101, 129, 135; communication of, 51–52, 62–63, 67; exercises, 55; and healing, 24, 25, 83–84; of natural cycles, 151, 152, 157; and soul loss, 59–60, 62–63, 176; transmutation of, 41–50, 61–62; using to create future, 85–86, 87–88
Eternity, focus on, 17, 169
Exercises, 20, 36–38, 78–79, 102–3, 124–25, 144–45, 158–59, 167

Fasting, and vision quests, 4–5
Fear, 53; of change, 107–8

Feelings: empathy for, 59–61; exercises, 54; and identity, 77; lack of, 31–32; and thought energy, 41–45
Fire: in nature, 149; in rituals, 89–98
Future, the, 175; creating, 1–2, 11, 35, 87–88; exercises, 20; Isis's version of, 14–17; journeying to, 46–50

Goals, 17, 33
Groups: finding support, 94–95, 96–97; healing community, 99–101; power animals of, 133; in rituals, 6, 89–90
Guilt. *See* Blame

Healing: asking for help in, 117–18; life after, 6, 13, 83–84; power animals in, 32–33, 59–60; process, 2, 30, 73, 115–18, 178; receiving, 27–29, 34–35; soul retrieval in, 23–29, 75; spontaneous, 26
Helping professionals, 62; and clients' focus, 6; taking care of themselves, 59–61, 64
Helping spirits, 46, 172; exercises, 55; finding one's, 69; help from, 24, 110, 117–18; in rituals, 31, 89–90, 176–77, 178–79; withdrawal of, 165. *See also* Isis; Power animals
History: clients', 24, 31–32; neighborhoods', 134–35. *See also* Past
Horwitz, Jonathan, 89
Humor, 53

Identity, 68, 73. *See also* Self-knowledge

Proudfoot–Edgar, Carol, 161
Psyche, and rituals, 88
Psychic littering, 45–47, 51
Psychic warfare, 51, 175–76
Psychology, vs. shamanism, 174
Psychopomps, shamans as, 178

Reality, 14; exercises, 20
Receiving: exercises, 36–37; healing, 25, 27–29, 34–35; information, 112–15, 154–55
Relationships, 119–20; being strong in, 72, 74, 76; exercises, 78–79; setting boundaries in, 67–68, 74
Releasing rituals: of negative beliefs, 88–99; of pain, 61–62
Responsibility: for choices, 1–2, 108, 132; for effects of energy, 41–45, 51; for health, 29–30, 34, 87–88
Rhythms, natural and personal, 157
Rituals: exercises, 102; releasing, 61–62, 88–98; to return stolen souls, 176–77; to transmute negative energy, 47–49. See also Soul retrieval

Safety, 27–28; for soul to return to, 26, 71–72, 175
Scarcity, 18, 150
Self-knowledge, 107–9, 112; of energy exchange, 62–63; exercises, 124, 125, 158; of feelings, 44–45, 61; of learning styles, 114–15; of rhythms, 152–54, 157
Senses, 28, 70, 113–15; exercises, 36–37
Service, in business, 130–32
Shaman, role of, 172–73, 177, 178

Shamanism, 3–4, 6, 89, 133–34, 171–79; guidance, 111, 113–15; healing, 60, 73, 87–88, 122. See also Journeying; Soul retrieval
Siempre, story of, 9, 163–65, 169
Silence, 18–19
"Song of Return (Soul Retrieval Poem)" (Proudfoot–Edgar), 161
Soul essences, 120, 121
Soul loss, 62–63; effects of, 177; of places, 136–42; reasons for, 23, 25–26, 68, 74–75, 174–75. See also Soul retrieval
Soul remembering, 118–21
Soul retrieval: effects of, 60, 68, 74, 76–77, 109–10; for places, 137–42; process, 23–29, 31–33, 177; and soul remembering, 118
Soul Retrieval: Mending the Fragmented Self (Ingerman), 62, 73, 94, 99, 109, 150–51
Soul stealing, 26, 73–74, 175–77
Spirits: of community, 135; exercises, 124; help from, 44, 132; information from, 110, 111; of nature, 154–55; trust in, 99. See also Helping spirits
Support: after healing, 89, 94–95, 100–101; lack of, 32
Symbols, in rituals, 89–90, 119–21

Talisman, in rituals, 89–90
Teachers: ancestors as, 137–39; descendants as, 46–49. See also Helping spirits; Isis; Power animals
Territories, in nonordinary reality, 172, 177

For information on workshops given by Sandra Ingerman and associates, please write:

Sandra Ingerman
P.O. Box 4757
Santa Fe, New Mexico 87502